Presented as a gift by
Robert R. Rosenheim
in memory of his parents
Harry and Ruth Rosenheim

The View From
My Rooftop

The View From My Rooftop

Reflections of an Inner Life

Renée Garfinkel

BIC Publishing
Washington, DC

The View From My Rooftop: Reflections of an Inner Life

Printed in the United States of America

For information address BIC Publishing
The National Press Building, 529 14th Street, NW
Washington DC 20045

To order copies of the book, e-mail: jygrfnkl@AOL.COM

To contact the author: Reneeg@erols.com

ISBN 0-9679428-0-2

First Edition

For Jay
and
Elon and Xeriqua
who make everything possible

Contents

Acknowledgements

So many people have helped me craft this work that I'm not sure I can mention them all.

Of primary importance are the people mentioned in this book, identified either by their initials or not at all. Since consciousness develops in its relationship to people, each of them helped shape this work.

I am grateful to those who gave their time, their support and commented on the manuscript: Jay Garfinkel, Katherine Whipple, Jonathan Groner and Suzanne Singer.

Marilyn Grossman designed the cover sketch. Mark Wright provided the graphic interpretation of the sketch and was the book designer. Marci Bloch made valuable proof reading suggestions.

The thing I like about birthdays is you don't have to earn them. On one day each year people tell you they are glad you exist. They are happy on this day because you appeared on the planet. They congratulate you for simply being alive. Just thinking about it makes me happy+-.

When I was a very little girl, I went under the staircase to think. The small dark space near the building's mailboxes was hardly noticeable to adults, but it was a cozy niche for me. People who came by to get their mail didn't even notice me until I startled them by saying hello. (Like servants and maintenance people, children enjoy the advantages of being invisible.)

On the whole, I think I was an agreeable child. At least that's what I've been told. I know I was a reflective one. Under the staircase I could be alone, to daydream and think without interruption. Under the staircase, I thought about thinking, and how I knew what I knew, and why things were the way they were. And who would I be if I weren't me? Life in my family was contentious, confusing, and sometimes frightening. It had great unhappiness at its core. But under the staircase, no one bothered me. I was alone to figure things out. I formulated my own ideas about the family dynamics and acted on them: who was weak and needed protection, who was to blame, who could be trusted and for what. I needed to figure it out. There was a subtext to everything, a shadow reality. So under the staircase I turned ideas around and around. In my imagination, my parents and relatives, and the people picking up their mail, became different from the way they appeared. I wondered why they did the things they did. I'd sit cross-legged in that little space, on a floor of small, hexagonal white tiles, with brown angular designs along the border - the kind you see in Spike Lee movies, or TV shows like *Brooklyn Bridge* - and wonder about the world. It was only much later that I learned words for what I saw and felt and thought about under those stairs.

Some children's minds are born when they lie in tall grass, staring at the clouds, others when they stare out to sea. My consciousness came to life in a nook in the dark, under a well-used staircase on East 21st Street.

I started out thinking under the stairs, and since then I've thought in many, many places. Some places are better for it than others. A swing in a playground, or a walking path by the water help move one's thinking along. So does being in a new place, and coming back home. I have had many such comings and goings. One could say that my thinking career began in the mailroom, on the ground floor, and it is now on the rooftop. When I was little I had a space under the stairs, now that I am fifty, I have a room of my own. I have a roof garden at home and a roof deck in the office. I have more time, and peace, as well as space for contemplation. And I have had a great deal of practice.

It's taken me a long time to climb up to the roof. The view from up here is wider than the one I had back then. And my thoughts have more words to ride on now. I write them in my journal so I can see what I think. In the seasons that have turned these many years I find that some of the things I think about have changed, although remarkably, many have remained the same.

When I was a little girl, I looked forward to my birthday and the gifts I would receive. Now that I'm turning 50, I still look forward to my birthday, but this time it's my turn to give a gift. A gift of myself, from my journal.

This, then, is the view from my rooftop. Here's how the world looks from where I sit.

Summer

I started my working life in earnest when I was 17. My father died that year, leaving me and my mother with no money at all. She had never worked outside the home. Throughout the many years of working for wages, getting up at 4 in the morning to spend dark hours in the cold and wet, my father made regular contributions to his pension fund. He was a scholar who earned his living working with his hands, and he looked forward to spending his retirement years in study. That was not to be. He died long before retirement age, losing all the value of his insurance, which did not transfer to his survivors. In 1967, as in the days of the Prophets of old, the powerful institutions - labor unions, pension managers, and the government - were indifferent to the needs of widows and orphans.

My serious working life began at 17. After working for thirty-odd years, it was time to take a Sabbatical year. Time simply to be, to think about things impractical. Time to contemplate and nurture my inner life. Time, in short, to listen to the music of life in a different key. In order to avoid a shock to my system, I decided to begin the Sabbatical gently, by taking the summer off. Or at least trying to take a complete day off in the middle of every week. The last full summer vacation I had was back in high school, and I wasn't sure I'd remember how to do it!

The idea of taking a year off sounds simple. I was surprised to learn that it was not.

The excerpts of my journal that follow are snapshots of my Sabbatical journey. Just before the Sabbatical my work life revolved around several activities. Gerontology Services (GS) was a consulting practice to nursing homes, rehab centers, and other institutions that dealt with the elderly. I employed up to 6 psychologists at a time, providing neuropsychological testing, training and education to the staff. I had a private psychotherapy practice. In addition, a couple of times a year I provided Disaster Mental Health (DMH) services during national disasters, such as earthquakes, floods, or airplane crashes.

Adoption Studies Institute (ASI) was an organization I had started a few years earlier, to add a voice of rational thinking to the hysterical and ideologically-driven field of adoption. Related to that, I founded the first peer-reviewed professional journal of adoption, *Adoption Quarterly* (*AQ*) and was its editor.

On the family side, after years of marginal survival in her own apartment, years of refusing assisted living and other alternative sources of support, my mother finally entered a nursing home. My children were in their early 20's, and increasingly out on their own. Jay and I could take a deep breath, look at each other, and relax. It was the perfect time for a Sabbatical.

Remember those back-to-school compositions about "What I Did on My Summer Vacation?" Here are excerpts from my notebooks, highlights of my trip to the interior.

1 June

June 1 is the "official" start of my sabbatical, at least in my head. And this sabbatical IS in my head, for there is no external difference that can be observed. I will come to the office most days, trying to invest myself in activities for reasons other than economic. It makes a great deal of difference in my head, but will hardly be visible to the casual observer. Gerontology Services, once successful beyond my expectations, has become a drag, with HMOs & managed care running interference. Private patients trickle in, sometimes more, sometimes fewer. I think they may increase. But I am trying gently to focus my efforts on the here and now.

It is so much harder to write - to experience myself and reflect on my experiences - at home than when away. I seem to need a lot of time alone with myself to really see both what's within and around me. At home I generate an internal sense of urgency, even when I seem relaxed. There are always tasks to be done, problems to address, or goals to be set and then accomplished. It's remarkably difficult to just be. Part of the resistance to just being is my ambivalence toward it: maybe the whole idea is just a way to escape having to make work/career decisions; maybe I'm just lazy and don't want to DO anything. Maybe I'm a failure for having nothing that I love doing.

This sabbatical thing is going to take some courage and perseverance. Maybe even some creativity.

3 June

I wish my hobby were collecting stamps, or pebbles. I would sit in the evenings at the dining room table examining the little round stones, arranging little pieces of colored glass in mounds that absorbed my attention. The collection's growth would mark the time I spent with it, the play of light through the hills of colored bits would please me softly. It would be art, and a monument to my hours. Instead I want to string little words in a line, pretty words, whose form reflects light in bits of truth. If only I could move words around like pebbles in a pile. They would have a life of their own, and I would be their admirer. Then I could just step back and watch my word piles grow with the gentle satisfaction of a collector with her hobby.

4 June

Rayshit chachmah yir'at Hashem - The beginning of wisdom is fear of God. It is generally understood to mean that recognition of authority precedes knowledge and understanding. I think it may also mean that the beginning of wisdom is that only God is to be feared. Nothing else. The understanding that nothing under the sun need be feared will free a person from the tyranny of anxiety, worry, even a good deal of anger and sadness. One may wish that unpleasantness not happen, but if fear is really only attached to God - who is eternal and steadfast - why worry?

5 June

My horoscope today said there would be a creative breakthrough, so I knew I had to take time;

Right after I conferenced with a therapist
Checked adoption records for a birth mother's address
Called Mom's internist
Did billing for ASI, GS, and Mom

I did take time... I did, I did
Before making the bank deposits
and getting cash for groceries,
Before balancing the account
and second-guessing the prescription
Before following up on services uncompleted

I took time for the gym.

An old man puffed by. "Boy, am I tired," he said,
"But your nice smile makes it worth it."

Horoscopes never lie.

16 June

Yesterday was Sunday June 15
Father's Day
Another Graduation Day
Mom's rent due
Our oldest friends' wedding anniversary (before they got divorced).
We bought a tree for our balcony.

I pedaled around Hain's point, past urban fishermen,
and family barbecues.
My dark-skinned neighbors relaxed in summer's Sunday sun,
and across the Potomac white folks did the same.

By the time I got back to catch the evening movie, the latest
hot-blooded epic of
violence
greed and
destruction,

I felt this summer vacation might really have a chance.

27 June

I feel like I've turned the corner to 50. I appreciate the trough of summer, the lull created as much by convention as by nature. I've begun to appreciate my casual good health, and the moments of calm well-being delight me as once only thrilling moments could. Breakfast with a friend is a luxury I once couldn't afford that has now become a priority.

I don't need to vacation to "get away", as one doesn't need to go to synagogue to pray. The elements that make vacations attractive are what I am in the process of integrating into my life.

With it all I have to admit that this sense of well-being, which expands silently like a balloon filling with air whenever I focus on it, derives its strength from my children's well-being. Watching them grow whole and well, independent and strong, trusting their delicate beauty to the world and its forces, is the base of well-being from which the rest grow. Flowers may not resemble the earth from which they spring, but their lives depend on the earth. I am grounded in the children's development, as I once was the ground for their development. Much as I admire philosophies of detachment, I know I need them to be OK. When they falter or suffer, I cannot distance myself from the hurt.

28 June

When I want to feel relaxed, is it a change in mood I seek, or am I trying not to hear what my brain is saying? It seems that I want to turn down the noise my brain generates, the obsessiveness with details, minutiae, the needs and deeds of people around me. It isn't always easy to be both awake and relaxed enough to focus on more central issues, or on nothing at all. Perhaps I should meditate and use the brain cells I have, rather than trying to chill them out.

Louis Jacobs' book of testimonies of Jewish mystics shows what hard work and discipline mysticism is, for Jews, Buddhists and anyone else. Master musicians of the spheres, they are the original soul men.

Can one interpret the Shema's admonishing "*lo toturu acharai l'vavchem v'acharai aynaychem...*"(Do not wander away following your heart and following your eyes) to be a call for detachment and correct focus? Focus on the mantra, the sound of Shema, and don't be distracted by the lure of the visual and the visceral.

July

1 July

Lunchtime today began with Erica behind the counter at Godiva Chocolatier, wearing an apron, laughing with her supervisor. A flower in a chocolate field. I took her recommended selections to Elon at the Chamber of Commerce editing room where he showed me the graphics he was working on for the show,*The Bull And The Bear*. He demonstrated how he can make the bulls pop up and disappear. He was focused, competent, and pleased with his handiwork. How satisfying to see them acting in the world; how fortunate we are.

10 July

Laurie Knapp, in her autobiography *Drinking: a love story*, writes about the ambivalence that was at the core of her addiction, and her father's life. All alcoholics lie, she claims. All have hidden lives, hiding the alcoholism most of all, and most of all from themselves. Perhaps that's true; substances help blur the painful edges of reality, and the deceptions involved in maintaining a secret life are sharp edges that pierce self esteem. But the lure of having a secret life is wider than alcoholism. The popularity of storylines involving a bland accountant who is a bigamist with two families who live in cities an hour apart testifies to that lure. Alan Alda's movie, *This Time Next Year*, has become a classic. The secret second life defies mortality. If you can have more than one life, then you cheat the system that has set that most awful limit, death. Ambivalence about commitment may be reluctance to confront the reality behind it, namely, that choosing door number one means you will never...NEVER...see what's behind doors 2 and 3.

14 July

Harriet is an attractive, fit, middle-aged woman who works out at the gym. She looks like a PBS ad, healthy and natural, with no makeup, thick gray hair, and a particularly American style of openness. She just came home from the Sundance ritual, 4 days of fasting and dancing with an American Indian tribe. She was the only Caucasian among the 90 dancers, whose sacrifice - in addition to abstaining from food and water for 4 days, sitting in the sweat lodge, and dancing in a sacred circle around the Tree of Life - included "piercing" by the men. This piercing involves sewing leather thongs through their skin and muscles, attaching the thongs to the tree, and dancing back from the tree until their flesh tears. Harriet went from late 20th century Christian Washington, DC to participate in a pagan ritual deplored by the Bible. It contained all the elements against which Judaism rebelled. Judaism was born in opposition to such practices and the ideas they represent - worship of natural phenomena like trees, tearing of flesh as a mode of worship, human sacrifice. The idea that one person's suffering can be exchanged for another's healing is utterly rejected. And how powerful these "forces" of ideas and wishes are - to to reach forward from primitive times and enchant a woman like Harriet!

16 July

What would happen if I wrote a complete thought every day? Not just a fragment of feeling or report on the moment, but a complete thought. In paragraphs, with a beginning, a middle, and an end. It would mean that I'd write for an hour or more. It would mean that I'd fill at least one whole page. It would mean that I'd read more thoughtfully, weigh more analytically, and ponder, and focus, attend and remember more purposefully. It would mean that when a year has gone by I'd have some three hundred pages of writing. I'd have spent the year writing. What an idea.

17 July

Ever since I wrote those words I've been struck dumb. I answer my e-mail in awkward, stilted sentences that remind me of my doctoral dissertation, damned by my advisor with the faint praise, "no excess verbiage". I procrastinate, delaying my other activities until there simply is no time to write. A complete thought a day? What WAS I thinking!? My mind is a blank. Resistance is alive and well.

18 July

Every species has its unique faculty that helps it survive: speed, a long neck, camouflage colors, or quills. Humans have their moral sensibility. Human societies gain internal strength and the clarity of vision required to defend themselves against outside enemies when they build their behavior and their institutions in a moral fashion. The "Monica Lewinsky matter" has dominated America all year. While we and our leadership spin excitedly over the prospect of a semen-stained dress, India and Pakistan explode nuclear weapons, the economies of Japan and the rest of Asia slide downward, and children in Washington, DC don't learn to read. Like so many things, it's about attention. And we are distracted.

19 July

I'm playing with a technique to lower emotional reactivity. When I become annoyed, irritated and impatient (whether with those I love or just the anonymous clerk at the other end of the line) I think, "Pretend it is tomorrow, or next Wednesday. How do I feel about this?" Most things will have been forgotten by that time, and the realization makes me smile. A smile's a gentle, effective weapon against the inner enemies, rage and fear.

20 July

I have too much experience with depression not to know

better. Surrounded by the effects of depression on the family as I was in my childhood, I ought to have grown a callus, or have had my heart hardened like Pharaoh. But depressions in those I love still terrify me. A lump the size of Nebraska forms behind my breastbone, taking up space between my heart and my throat, my gut and my lungs. It is a cancer that steals my appetite and leaves me nauseated. My spine turns to liquid. Breathing becomes harder. All I want to do is save them. I would pull them from the black waves like a lifeguard, like a firefighter I would beat back the approaching ooze that sucks the color and life from their world. I would shift into overdrive, whirl like a dervish, grow extra arms to keep them safe...if only I could. The abyss threatens to engulf them - and me along with them.

I take a walk, eat some ice cream, think obsessively of helpers to call or avenues to explore. My mind tiptoes around the corners of my fears, of the nameless plagues that can strike under the cover of despair, where even the hope of light is extinguished.

22 July

I used to work so much harder. I never used to have a day like today, when I have both the pace and the space to be conscious of my time as it goes by. Although I have always been a reflective person, there were many years, beginning, perhaps, in graduate school in Denmark, or maybe before, that I was more reactive and emotion-driven than I ever realized. "Chased by the man with the gun", I called it. It meant more than economic necessity. It meant living life driven by fear, a nameless, faceless fear of both abandonment and engulfment, of falling into lives like the ones I saw around me, of missing out or being left behind if I didn't stay on track. It was a fear built on the lost lives of women, and the uneasy lot of Jews. It was a fear of my mother's demons, my father's helplessness, and the lack of something to count on. Everyone was limited. God didn't know what He was doing, or if He did, He wasn't telling. In the madness and maelstrom that was the human condition, it was truly remarkable that sometimes people were kind and true, and put another's needs before their own. If they didn't, and weren't...well, who could blame them? Look at what they had to deal with! It seemed natural to be frightened. It seemed smart. If it kept one focused and alert, then fear was not so bad, I thought. When I thought about it at all. Now, on a sultry Wednesday in July, I have spent hours being aware and appreciative of the hours. Today I encouraged an *AQ* author, and discussed his issues of interest. I wrote e-mail about the synagogue hospitality program, perused vegetarian websites, I wrote to B. about getting together; she who returned from the mouth of the monster after her terrible car accident, miraculously without intellectual damage, but with a useless hand. I read Ramachandran & Sandra Blakeslee's *Phantoms in the Brain* and enjoyed a solitary lunch at the Mexican place across the street. Nachos and a soggy salad with pumpkin seeds. Mediocre food, and a little change of location was all I needed.

For many years Mom would spend all day and night alone. It would take her all morning to get dressed and "straighten up," for her outing to a coffee shop for a lunch of bagel and coffee. Some days she would get to her group, or a doctor's appointment at Coney Island Hospital. She'd have her coffee there, and, with apologies about kashrut, a bagel, too. It would take all day, including all the time spent waiting for busses. By the time she returned home in the late afternoon she'd be exhausted. That was all she did, and I felt so sorry for her. She was usually depressed, frequently paranoid, childishly embroiled in her relationship with her sister, and she often hallucinated. In those days, in her early 60s, she was still able to censor her conversations with and about the voices she heard. Perhaps now she would look back on those years as having been good. I will ask her about it when I visit this coming Sunday.

I look on these years as being very good. I have so many layers of cushion and support, which shape a soft, pleasing life. More and more I can taste the food I eat, hear the music I listen to, feel the air that I move through. I am aware that most of the time my body feels good. Sometimes there are throbs and aches, but they remain below a level of concern. I generally experience my body as straight, whole and rested. Most mornings I sleep until I wake up naturally, a unique blessing in itself. On a day like today, I am even aware of feeling refreshed as my blood sugar rises after lunch. I believe I even feel myself digesting! Awareness like this reminds me of a child at a carnival, pointing in every direction, because everything is interesting, remarkable and fresh. A deeper, quieter pleasure has replaced the childish excitement, but otherwise it is much the same. Like the child, I feel cared-for and protected: Jay pays the bills, Rosa does the laundry, our stocks keep going up. Like the child, I am mostly unpressured. There is not much that I have to do that I don't want to do. And when there is, I can usually put it off for later. Good things just happen, and I enjoy them, like T. coming along to the supermarket, or S. inviting us out to dinner-happily on the evening the A/C went out. Without stress I can be like the child, in the moment.

And like a child my nerves are tender, sensitive. Not every moment is good. The next moment the phone rings, disturbing the tranquil silence, demanding attention. It was Jay, who became impatient - irritated - with my slow consideration of the problem he presented. So I hurried, and produced an approach to the problem, the way a child shaken from her reverie will attend to the chore: dutifully. I hung up a little shaky, and a little angry, more at the fragility of the mood I had been so proud of than at Jay's unwitting disturbance of it. The silk sheet I had spent all day smoothing and admiring now lay carelessly rumpled, disregarded. I had mistaken my pretty pile of pillows for a fort.

24 July

The weakness of my eyes saddens me. The left one can't be fully corrected at all. Seeing my vision deteriorate makes me feel my mortality. My eyes are healthy, there is no explanation for the loss. It is depressing to think that it will simply continue to decline. Jay's father is blind. For me, a person who reads as naturally as she breathes, visual loss is particularly poignant. At least I live in an age of talking books, voice mail, and increasingly vocal computers. Still, when I looked at the line on the eye chart and saw nothing...barely smudges against the white wall...I felt sadly vulnerable.

25 July

I am easily distracted from the sadness about my eyes - even just by the gym, or condo board business. But when the distractions leave, my mood falls again. And I am classically irritable. (Telephone clerks who ask me questions instead of responding to mine are sandpaper on tender flesh - I want no one to ask me for anything.) It didn't help to learn that Johnson & Johnson doesn't even make a disposable bifocal lens in my strength! The whole business is very sobering. I feel like I am moving from nearsightedness to low vision. It threatens to be a doorway into patient-hood. Disability. Do I resist, or let the feelings do their thing as I watch, and they dissolve? Where does "letting it be" end and "wallowing" begin?

But I felt fine, even honored, when a colleague poured out her story about meeting her birth father, the man who abandoned her mother when she was pregnant. Praised for my suggestions in a public forum, I recognized that the approval meant too much to me. Preoccupation with my vision has thinned my skin even more.

Still, this reminder of mortality is an opportunity. An especially good opportunity if all it ends up being is merely a stronger lens prescription, nothing worse. If it does end up being worse, I'll still need to learn from and with it. That's the message.

26 July

Thinking ahead to my 50th birthday, I'd like to tell my family & friends what I have learned:

I began my career in gerontology because I wanted to see what becomes of people as they travel through life. It was a way of examining the good life. More than most young people, I had a chance to observe, contemplate, and read about many lives lived. From my point of view, with the privilege of being allowed into the inner lives of individuals and families, many ordinary lives revealed their radiance in their struggles, challenges, even their regrets. I recognized the importance of being who you are. So I am going to share with you who I am at 50.

I have always lived in my head, which is an interesting address, but often has the effect of distracting me from what is right in front of my face. Being who you are means experiencing what is. Being an artist means being able to express it. Lately I've learned to focus somewhat better, by asking myself, "what do I mean right now?" What I mean - being able to say precisely what one means - is the hallmark of good art, good writing - because it is a good way of being.

I've learned that the good life is lived in many ways, all of them marked by altruism and an emphasis on something bigger than and outside of oneself. It is hard to live a good life when one is insecure, fearful of the future in any way. When I was 16, I asked the middle-aged bus driver at day camp a question: what did he want to look back on when he was old? He answered simply, "I spend time with people I like, I avoid contact with people I don't, and in the evenings I play in a band." He seemed happier, more relaxed and younger than other people his age. I have since asked hundreds of people the same question, and have come to recognize the said and unsaid elements in the answer. People who can make their art or hobby continue into their later years are especially blessed.

So are those who have come to terms with control. So much time and energy is wasted in relationships where one is afraid of what will happen if they don't control the other. Or the other is afraid of being controlled. Being what one is, and being able to say so, risks having your needs refused (ignored, rejected, manipulated). Living well means taking that risk, and sometimes losing.

I've learned that often keeping up a good front drives others away, because the glue holding that front in place has a bad smell. It smells false. I've learned that complaining is a habit, a social convention, that also leaves a scent on the people and places in which complaining takes place. Complaints bond as well as alienate, particularly if the litany ends with a self-effacing laugh. I learned that from a very good friendship back in junior high.

Speaking of junior high, I've learned all along the way that older is better. The additional spaces that open inside as one travels through time are places made of experiences of love. There are gradations of feelings that become more nuanced with the years, softening the painful sound and fury that is the emotional reality of even the most outwardly composed young person. I've begun to understand, even if I sometimes forget, that everything I do and feel and think is ephemeral. I may not even remember the moment that seems ultimately important today. But that very evanescence only increases the importance of the good I may do.

Because I understand that the pain that lays me low today is gone without a trace tomorrow, I can feel the importance of the homeless person's hunger. I take a moment to look in his face when I hand him a box of raisins. I hope it relieves his pain for a moment. This moment is all we have.

When the landlord imposed a heavy rent increase, I moved my office. I hated having to move, but like so many unplanned events, the move turned out to be in my best interests.

27 July

I spent today meeting with the mover and the hauler. Carlos the mover is from Peru and is studying for a Master's degree in Public Policy. Only in Washington! Latif the hauler asked the same question as Carlos when they learned that I was a shrink: how do you deal with hearing all that heavy stuff? How do you sleep at night? Their question pleased me.

28 July

The crusher is coming to haul and destroy all Gerontology Services records. Years and years of patients served. The files of their testing, testament to their injuries and sorrow, their pain. The deadpan description of their histories, their families. Perhaps they live forever in God's memory, as each is one of His children, impossible to forget. But the trace they made on my memory is fading, and in a few days their records will be mulch. I feel lighter just thinking about their disposal. It is better to travel light

30 July

I am weary with anemia and cramps of my period. It's a useless, messy, unpleasant few days that soon won't be part of my life, and I wonder what that will be like. My post-menopausal friends don't seem older than me; with estrogen replacement no one has facial hair, coarse skin or sagging breasts, but what does it mean no longer to have a rhythm inside your womb that's been silently measuring the months since earliest adolescence? The menstrual cycle is like a heartbeat or pulse, part of the ongoing music of a person's life, occasionally making itself noticed and reminding me of the internal symphony to which I am oblivious, and for which I am grateful. These dragging days of my period may be among my least favorite tunes, but menopause is a program note announcing that one day all the music will stop.

August

2 August

It's the third day of my allotted week for settling in. The

office is adorable. It's a fantasy, having a study, a room of one's own, just down the street from home. It amuses me to walk into the lobby and greet the custodian, the guardian of this place of my own. (His name, Wendell Fraser, strikes me as delightfully formal for a man in his position). The room is bookish, and spare, with good light coming from the quiet alley behind. Regardless of what kind of work will emerge from this space, I feel so lucky to have it.

The aggravation of real life is compressed and magnified by moving. It's frustrating. Of course I am aware of how insignificant these obstacles are compared to real problems in the world (the future of a disabled child, for example; the challenges that face an abled child; or yesterday's earthquake in Turkey that killed at least 1,000 people, and injured thousands more). But hours spent on the phone with anonymous, incompetent clerks, techs and salespeople are hours of my lifeblood seeping away. It drips out of my vein, pale pink with exhaustion, as my other hand desperately holds the receiver. I grow weaker. I'm on hold.

These days are secret treasures. By mid-month, August will begin to fall - faster and faster as it descends into September. Washington is quiet. Congress - therefore everyone - is out of town. Camp and school are out, too, so parents take off with their children. On days like today city lovers like me are in their element. We are like camp counselors left behind when all the campers have gone home. We finally have the place all to ourselves.

Most people are gone. Others, my academic colleagues, are busy preparing for the school year to begin. It seems that I alone bear witness to these days.

3 August

There is also something depressing about turning the corner into August. The deep silence that will fall over Washington this month liberates parking spaces, but hints that September is on its way. Today business as usual began to roll in: some *Gerontology Services* referrals, bank and Medicaid snafus, manuscript pushing for *AQ*. When the first issue finally appeared, like a baby born after 11 months of gestation, it was pleasing to see, but long overdue. I would have been more excited to see it 6 months earlier. Now that it's become more routine, the journal represents "work" almost (but not quite) as much as it represents the actualization of an idea.

4 August

When I pay close attention to my experience, it is almost more than I can bear. A little "bug" that makes me queasy and pains my head turns the universe a color of swirling, sickening aqua-grey color. I am like an infant, my sensations ARE the world. Although I may know better, my reality is no less comprehensive. I feel sick, and the world of before or after, happy or well times are as if they never happened. They can't even be imagined. Such is the influence of body on mind.

I walked to work trying to meditate, bringing my mind back from its wanderings . When I succeed, for only moments at a time, to be aware of myself and my surroundings, I feel like screaming at the intensity of stimulation. Is there always so much incoming sensation? How much energy must it be taking to keep it all out! The dappled sunlight on the sidewalk, the bright summer clothing of the people walking by, the traffic under the M Street bridge, the man walking his dog. There was Earl the panhandler, in new checkered Bermuda shorts, his sign with the misspelled "pless" (please). In the bright, noonday sunlight it is all too intense, and I duck into the ice cream store for a Coke to quench my thirst and ease my still-present nausea.

Maybe it's all just a migraine.

5 August

The best part of today was asking the clerk at Barnes & Noble for Annie Dillard's books and having another customer turn toward me with a fond smile. "I love her work. *The Writing Life* is the best!" "Oh, yes", I enthused, "smart writers are a pleasure. Have you read her latest book, *For the Time Being?* I took it out of the library." It was on his to-do list.

That was the most personal face-to-face conversation I had today with anyone outside of my family. And it felt personal, since we both feel like intimate friends of Annie Dillard. Now that's being a writer.

6 August

Connection and separation, are the two poles that make possible the electrical energy of life. Anticipating Tisha B'Av this week I recall that the cause of destruction and Diaspora is *Sinat chinom*, causeless hatred. The key word here is "causeless." When religious folks hate they convince themselves that they are like Pinchas, jealous for God's sake. I don't think God needs all that defense, He can take care of himself. Hating for the sake of integrity, or because another's ideas are in themselves harmful makes sense. But I would like to convince Jewish factions that there is so much common ground. In fact, were it not for the political labels of Orthodox, Conservative, Reform, etc. we could see that some folks, regardless of label, are better at certain Mitzvot than others. Then we could admire the Lakewood Yeshiva boy's attention to *shatnez* (the prohibition against wearing a garment made of wool and linen), rather than deride his compulsiveness. And we would honor contributors to Jewish communal or educational welfare, without referring to their personal observance. If someone gets to a destination by a different road, is he not a fellow traveler? Even if we're traveling for different reasons, isn't it the same wind at our backs?

But if we believe that our way is best, then the others are wrong or mistaken. And if we believe that all ways are good, just some more suitable to me and others to you, then we don't stand for anything. Therein lies the tension between separation and connection in this arena. Some resolve it by "love the sinner, hate the sin" compromise. Others, like Rav Kook, hold a "liberal" position that upon close examination is condescending in its "tolerance." No one wants to be "tolerated" like a noisy, sloppy neighbor. We all want to be respected and accepted. In an ideal world we'd find something to accept and respect in each other. (Short of admiring the Nazis for making the trains run on time, or Farrakhan for promoting Black self-reliance. Some evils eclipse any good they may produce. And so we return to the splitting of separation)

Connection and separation are forces in adoption as they are in so much of life. The adoptee has been compared to a twig grafted onto another tree. But I think of the adoptee's life as a tributary flowing into the river of a new family and people. Is the water "really" the tributary or the river? Of course it is both, and neither. The strand of hair in a braid is not severed from its root. It has grown from there to participate in something larger than itself. It becomes braid, but never loses its individuality.

Our children are separating, slowly and palpably. Learning to relate to them as adults takes time, restraint and thought. They appear to want us to be available and supportive, on their terms. And their terms at this stage are to encourage, without pushing. Pushing, suggesting, implies criticism, and despite their bravado, their buds of independence are exquisitely sensitive. I'm very proud of them.

7 August

The secret of secrets is ineffable. It is connection.

And God? Well, He is eternal, and whatever is eternal is God. In our relationship with Him lies our eternity. We see it as a Covenant. Christians see it as incorporating the body of His son. Buddhists see it as experiencing the interrelatedness of all, the no-self Self, the expansion of the moment that fills the emptiness with joy and serenity. All seem to agree that it is in and through a connection with the eternal (rather than separation from it, or individuation into one's unique self) that one lives forever.

In the meantime, God, please protect my children. Help them grow whole and straight, to find their right connections.

Tonight is Tisha B'Av. It is a tragedy I don't know quite what to make of. Reading Jeremiah, I conclude that Jews are no worse than anyone else. Sure, we could be better and we should. The unjust society will collapse of its own accord, the Prophets tell us. Factions and divisiveness have done us in. The Rambam blamed neglect of the art of statesmanship. All societies decline and die, all civilizations disappear. Judaism is eternal, and its message as well as the sounds of its suffering echo forever. Perhaps those pains were not worse than the terminal sufferings of others who have devolved into silence. It does not matter whose were worse. What matters is that there continues to be the opportunity to do better. Judaism holds the promise of hope. Inspiring the idea of the possibility of perfecting oneself and society, inventing the human-Godly joint venture miracle of repentance, Judaism has to be eternal to be eternally perfectible. As a child I argued that a short happy life was better than a long, miserable one, but I know now those are not the two choices.

The Sephardi reading of Eicha (the book of Lamentations) includes a moment of drama in which all lights are turned off, and the reader notes the number of years since the destruction of the Temple in Jerusalem. The moment enacts and recalls the Spanish Inquisition, a turning point in

Sephardi history. Remembering in the dark. Mourning and performing rituals in the dark. We are no more modern than they, the Jews of Spain 500 years ago. Just the previous night Jay and I had been called for a Shiva minyan in the home of our downstairs neighbor. Her 52 year old daughter died. The "minyan" included Jews and gentiles of both sexes. The mourners could not read or follow, stumbling over the transliteration of Kaddish. The service consisted of a paragraph here, a selection there. A little responsive reading of a psalm, and a moment of silent prayer. Jay was recruited into leadership, supported by M., our contentious neighbor. But the ragtag minyan and the flimsy service seemed to comfort the bereaved mother. She cried and hugged. Her son, cordial and friendly in that Washington native-son way (soft southern accent, warm, touching-freely, thanking us for coming as he would at any reception), seemed disconnected from the reality that brought us there. He had just buried his sister. His father died long ago. He was all his mom had left.

Tisha B'Av

If God is a father, then he is an abusive one. His punishment, extended and entirely out of proportion, and His failure to protect his children from harm would justify Termination of Parental Rights in any decent society. Job clearly asserts that individual suffering is not a function of personal sin. Neither has the suffering of Israel been deserved.

I fast today in sympathy with, in memory of, that long history of suffering. Fasting declares my solidarity with Jews in every epoch whose difficulties echo in the Eicha lament. The kinot (elegiac poetry) are too painful to recite for long;

it is easier to fast. Fasting creates a space in which to see everyday frivolity. How needy and fragile we really are, when skipping a morning cup of decaf leaves a hole, and the day ahead looms off-balance because there will be no lunchtime and no dinner ritual. The day is distorted and abnormal long before I feel actual hunger, thirst, or weakness! My sticky mouth and occasional lightheadedness and heavy body movements of fasting did their job. I was constantly reminded of Tisha B'Av, as my day rolled by, in contrast, with its richness and variety.

9 August

Buddhism deals with how people suffer, Judaism wonders why. Job gets no answer to explain his suffering. He is merely assured that God cares about his creatures, and Man is to remain loyal to the Path. That is the answer as well to Kohelet's (Ecclesiastes) despair. "Be soothed, God loves you. Have faith, keep going on the path." That is the message meant to give meaning and comfort to the one floundering species that worries about such things.

10 August

It is noon today, the funereal mood of the 9 days and Tisha B'Av has lifted and I feel the upward curve of "Nachamu" (comfort) August is everywhere, the newspapers write articles about the inane topics of newspaper articles! My office phone is silent, my hours uncommitted. I still have to resist the impulse to fill the time with tasks and rush into projects I don't care for, but the impulse is growing weaker with familiarity.

11 August

R, a professor in the department of religion, responded to my idea of teaching a course in the psychology of religion by musing about how it probably belongs in the psychology department. I remembered all I disdain about academia.

12 August

I'm reading *Writing as Healing*, and Jan Philip Reemtsma's account of his kidnapping, *In The Cellar*. He reports writing it as a way of combating the enforced intimacy between him and his abductors. Oddly, making his ordeal public was a way of taking back his life. It made his trauma a part of his life, neither a self-contained event nor the whole of his life. Integrating the trauma.

13 August

A few bright-hot days in Paradise Island, Nassau, the Bahamas, settled in a comfortable condo with no choices to make but where to recline. That was our summer vacation. Spy novels and detective stories occupied eye and brain, which otherwise focused on the clean sweep of beach, its blue water so clear and artfully accented with sails, yachts and occasional jet skis it seemed a postcard stretched around to

360 degrees. Parasails floated in the sky, proclaiming a life of ease. Palm trees and pine trees coexisted, and oversized tropical flowers happily gave up their brief lives to please us with their color. Outside of Paradise Island, the island is poor, its vegetation scraggy. Native fruits, knaps and sugar apples, can only be bought from stalls in Potters Cay, sold by perhaps the poorest, who seem unfriendly as they strain to understand our English. Some vendors seem stoned, or maybe it was just the oppressive, punishing heat. To work outside daily, with only the shade of the bridge to counter the unrelenting sun, is to live in hell next door to paradise. Nassau is a tropical isle, abundant in slot machines, tourists, and salt water.

The underwater landscape is a metaphor for life. Fish swim busily by, displaying a sense of mission. They travel in schools, living in complex social arrangements chosen for safety and survival. They come in colors, they have strategies for protection and mutual assistance. And everything moves to the silent music of the waves. Snorkeling among them, I am relaxed by the scene. In the silent beauty, each unfamiliar form is another manifestation of the wonder of life. The tiny sliver darting by is a variation of its full-sized purple and yellow cousin. They are both obviously only a step removed from plants growing around them, with corals and sponges half-steps in between. The reef reminds me of the Mojave Desert: rock and cacti, and swirled formations that might just as easily be stones or bones, as corals. The Grand Canyon and the Arava were once under water, as one day this reef might be dry. I float around it in my mask, and I am part of the scene. What the fish are, what the plant, the sponge and coral are, I am, too. I have floated here forever, bearing witness.

16 August

I may be beginning to get in tune with my new rhythm. When I missed the opportunity to be part of the team that responded to the plane crash in Guam because I couldn't leave immediately, I relaxed. I was disappointed to miss (for now, at least) a real adventure, but it gave me 10 days to work on *Adoption Quarterly*, pay my bills at the end of the month, and not feel pressured. The trick is to feel pressured by neither demands nor the lack of them.

18 August

The Washington Post, CNN, ABC News, a *Washington Post* columnist, channel 9, *Time* magazine - the flurry of calls from the media is flattering. In only a few years of working in the adoption field I've become an "expert" to reporters who eat up experts in sound bites. Thirty minutes on the phone appears as a one-line quote, the only negative statement I uttered ("What the parties should avoid is... conflict and acrimony..."). Babies switched at birth are more interesting than this week's episode of the White House scandal, or Albanians fleeing the fighting in Kosovo, or Iraq refusing to disclose the location of its chemical cache. Thinking about them is less disturbing than thinking about the children starving in Sudan, victims of a conspiracy between drought and the military.

So I do my best in the interviews, enjoying the attention as one might a summer breeze. Notice it, smile, and move on.

20 August
Academic Conference
Minneapolis

I feel I have outgrown this kind of conference. Academics deal not with wisdom, but with data. Cumulative knowledge, and the games people play with it. Nice enough people, I guess, but not very interesting. Smart, educated, but not particularly wise. There is too little laughter here, and too much concern with practicality. Grants. Tenure. Publication dates. I see an occasional flash of cleverness, a whisper of creativity, but no brilliance. It will soon be time for me to move on.

But not today. Today I call S. and her husband, strangers who are friends of friends, who offer to show me around town. They show me the sculpture garden and the conservatory, and we drive around one of the lakes. M. teaches Jewish Studies in a small college 60 miles from town. His interest is Jewish spirituality and meditation. He suggests that Jewish meditation is different from Buddhist or mainstream meditation in that the aim of Jewish meditation is "d'vakut" - getting closer to God. The aim of other meditation is the self. I suggest that aiming at d'vakut is for the self as well. I silently consider the similarity: quieting the ego makes one more receptive. Meditation makes one open, available—available for what? That probably depends on one's culture. A Buddhist, sufficiently open, becomes enlightened. A Jew, when sufficiently attentive, is embraced by God. Aren't they probably the same? The similarity was obvious to me, but the conversation went no further. We walked on, and I saw big houses, lush lawns, a neighborhood of classic American prosperity. "It's pleasant," S. says when I ask her how she likes it here. "It's not Jerusalem, so what's the difference where we are? It's Galut." We weren't a perfect match, but I am grateful for their hospitality. I am a little less a stranger here because of them.

23 August

R.M.'s presentation on transracial adoption depressed me this morning. Biracial children are black, she said, because they are treated as black. Black children need special consideration to be able to fit in somewhere in this racist society. Hearing this talk the day after the arrest of the man who shot up the JCC in L.A. was too much for me. He told police that shooting little children at day camp was " a wake up call to America to say that it's time to kill the Jews."

The gunman was known to the psychiatric system, to whom he confessed a wish to hurt others and be shot by the police himself. He was jailed for threatening psych staff with a knife. He's been involved with Aryan Nation or some other Nazi group since the early '90s. Lots of people, institutions and authorities knew this man was going to blow. The Nazis gave him a rationale and a target. And we have to find children families of their own race to help them learn to fit in. With this?

This is where our society is as we enter the 21st century. It's depressing to be so backward.

24 August

Perhaps anti-Semites hate Jews not for the usual reasons. We trot out the usual suspects: we are the conscience of the world, and resented for it. Or we are the chosen people, and resented for it. Or, having been exiled and stripped of all power, anti-Semitism is the quintessential blaming of the victim (a blaming which, I must hasten to add, we do ourselves. Take a look at the Siddur). I think there may be another reason. Jews embody another existential truth: that life is a permanent state of transit. Although we may long for home (God or The One, symbolizes the idea of being someplace, happy and peaceful, once and for all), the only living we can do is in transit. Judaism has made an art of it. Maintaining the fundamental faith in unchangingness, both at the beginning and at the Messianic end of the story, we focus our efforts on bringing drops of that unchangingness (holiness) into our trip. We sprinkle our journey with fairy dust, but it doesn't make us Peter Pan. We can't fly. Like everyone else on the planet, with or without a homeland, Jews are travelers. We just don't deny it.

When I get home I'm going to row on the Potomac.

I miss working out. I miss just sitting outdoors. I have so many outdoor spaces available to me now: the balcony and roof garden at home, the patio and roof in my new office. There is something about being outside that is so inviting.

I haven't checked my e-mail all week. I don't miss that. Minneapolis doesn't inspire. Neither do social science researchers. I seem to be looking for inspiration, or, failing that, at least a robust sense of humor. Neither was much in evidence this week. Just good, sincere people, some plodding forward, some thinking a little more widely. But wit is quicker, and erudition more prominent, at the Kemp Mill book club.

Tomorrow, after my talk, I will walk and walk around the University. I will walk by the river until I feel I have meditated. Until I feel that I have taken full advantage of this week away from home, in a new place. Until I feel that I will return home refreshed. I have felt too tired too much of the time here, and so have many other conference attendees. Hours of sitting and listening and concentrating leave the brain feeling saturated, the body crampy and stiff, the will sluggish.

25 August

Being away from home and community highlighted Shabbat as a spiritual practice. When more people observe Shabbat there is support for the discipline, but there is also the false veneer of social conformity. Judaism is particularly vulnerable to this confounding of motivations and outcomes because its spiritual practices are so rich, and they are knitted into the fabric of everyday life. Colors of everyday life, sometimes drab, sometimes sickening, bleed into the fabric. The resulting product is not pristine. One easily comes to blame the practice (and its source) for the practitioners' flaws. The practicing Jew faces the challenge of maintaining separation (kedushah) while walking through messy real life. We are directed to keep clean in the mud of economic, psychological, sexual and aggressive reality. Other religious systems let you withdraw in space. Judaism invites you to withdraw in time, but always in the company of intimates and acquaintances. "Detach without fleeing!", it challenges. "Here's how." Everything in creation is an opportunity. The difference between small issues and large may be an illusion (just as there is no up and down in space, no before and after in the Torah). Everything matters. The message gets lost in the noise of the community in which it is received. That noise includes all of human motivation: fear, aggression, subterfuge, selfishness. Everything shows up in the religious arena: competition ("look who thinks he's nothing!"), duplicity, power, rebellion, sex. Desire, longing, need. Fear. Loneliness.

26 August

The hardest part of living seems to be dealing with the unseen.

Proselytizers are almost funny in their conviction that what they know and believe to be true is not only universally true, but is also all that is needed. That is their arrogance. Moses' famous humility is probably not just a function of his recognition of his own limitations —after all, how could a man who had a face-to-face relationship with God NOT be impressed with his relative puniness? I think his renowned humility is more evident in the fact that he recognized how much he did not know. When the daughters of Zelofchad brought him their problem, he did not hesitate to consider anew that particular aspect of his lawgiving. He took his father-law's advice about public administration and governing. His humility appears in his openness and his willingness to reconsider and reflect. Moses was not known for his intelligence, his wisdom, or even his judgment. Rather, he was chosen for leadership after displaying empathy for the oppressed, an abiding sense of justice, and the courage to act.

27 August

Perhaps in retrospect this will have been the apex of Jewish life in America. This morning's *New York Times* featured an ad for Rosh Hashanah cards from Tiffany's. Page 3 of the *Times*: a tasteful card with the line, in Hebrew, *Lishanah Tovah Umitukah*. Twenty-five engraved cards for $90.

Graffiti warning, "Jews get out or be killed" was found on Ave. I in Brooklyn, in the heart of the largest, most identified Jewish community in the Diaspora. A Jewish high school student in Mississippi was forbidden to wear his Jewish star necklace because it might be mistaken for a gang symbol. The ACLU is fighting that front. What did you do when the Nazis began to organize, Grandma?

28 August

In youth, one learned to read the signs: letters, words, sentences, paragraphs. Then one learned to read between the lines. Truth, it seemed, was to be found in words and their juxtaposition, or in objects and their relationship. Now I see that to find truth, one must learn to read the white space on the page, since the most important message is hidden in what isn't there. The painting only makes sense if negative space is explored. That's why Buddhism has a message.

29 August

A trip to the beach reminded me once again of the unique satisfaction that is the pleasure of old friends; people who know you thoroughly, and accept you with all your foibles. Our children are now about the same ages now that we were when we met in Hackensack, united by our tentative first inquiries into the world of adoption. Of the four of us, only Jay has changed substantially since that time. The rest of us are pretty much the same as we were then. More experienced, certainly, and more accomplished, perhaps more self-assured, but essentially the same people. So I guess that is how our children will be, too. As they are today - with all their charms and limitations.

In *Through the Looking Glass*, Lewis Carrol has Alice frustrated in her attempt to get to the top of the hill. No matter which path she takes, they all lead her back to the house: "...but how curiously it twists! It's more like a corkscrew than a path! Well, this turn goes to the hill I suppose - no, it doesn't! This goes straight back to the house! Well then, I'll try it the other way." But try as she might, the paths seem to conspire against her, even seeming to twist and shake themselves to place her back at the front door. No matter what she tries, the house keeps getting in her way.

No matter where you go, there you are.

The beach - with no TV, radio, or computer, no crowds, not much to do, and the soothing balm of old friends - worked on my nerves the way its sand worked on my feet, rubbing away some of the callus, gently exposing the soft skin underneath. Perhaps we will visit there more often.

30 August

The Suicide Seduction

The author of *The Social Health of America* noted that teenage suicide has been rising steadily since 1970 (his baseline year). I wondered if it might be related to the media's constant conspiracy theme.

TV, movies and common wisdom – i.e., the "wisdom" of astrologers and psychics, UFOs, confirm a sense of the individual as helpless in an overwhelming, pervasive, hidden and malignant world. Kafka is everywhere. The 60's "don't trust anybody over 30" could identify the authority against whom to rebel. And you knew what they were doing: waging war in Viet Nam, perpetuating poverty and racism. And you knew why: profit, mostly. Now the enemy is vague: "government" or "democrats" (if you're a dittohead), "the machine" in the movie *Matrix*. And the *X files* - a series based on all the things the government is hiding, for ambiguous reasons. Hiding information is an end in itself: information is power. But maybe all this suspicion and cynicism makes alienated youth feel helpless and hopeless enough to kill themselves.

Or maybe it's just the reduced stigma against suicide. Kevorkian, assisted suicide in Oregon, hyperindividualism (Whose life is it, anyway?), weakened family ties. Maybe it's a reflection of the global increase in depression. *Lo hamaytim y'halleluyah* (the dead cannot praise God): death worship is a theme in pagan culture and in this one. Satanism and death images are deep in the culture's psyche, beginning just below the surface. Remember the fantastic child abuse cases in the early '90's? People went to jail because entire communities believed that Satanic rituals, sacrifices and practices were being performed on children in day care centers. National hysteria was aroused to such a pitch that professionals, even the so-called perpetrators themselves, were convinced! The persuasive power of very old, irrational ideas inflamed by modern context (our ambivalence toward children - we want to protect them, sure, but their abuse and humiliation is titillating) and promoted with modern technology—is staggering.

Eighties rock music used to bother me with all its skulls, despair and death symbolism. The survey said one out of four teenagers has thought about suicide seriously enough to consider a plan. One out of four - it's almost routine. Our children are killing themselves quietly. They kill each other with a lot of fanfare. How very sad for us all.

31 August

Happiness

I want to write some words about happiness, a subject that I have had an interest in throughout my professional career, but which has only just now moved up to the front of organized psychology's concern. Gerontology has always been concerned with life satisfaction (forms A & B). The Affect-Balance scale was a small but remarkably reliable instrument that recognized two separate emotional scales: positive and negative affect that were not, as common sense might have assumed, poles of the same dimension. Old people typically have a little less positive affect than younger ones, but they don't have more negative affect. People don't become less happy in old age. The cross-national differences in reported happiness have to be looked at skeptically. Scandinavians report higher levels of happiness than Southern Europeans. But I remember my Danish colleague who informed me that when a Dane answers how's it going? with "Meget godt" ("Very good!") it means "hal skidt" ("shitty")!

We now know that the left prefrontal cortex is busier in happy people than in miserable ones. Science is excited. *The New York Times* reported it. Doesn't everyone realize that the smile muscles are also more active in happy people. Does smiling therefore make people happy? As it happens, it does. Hence the character on Ally McBeal whose stiff-lipped smile doesn't match his eyes. "Smile therapy," he explains earnestly.

A good part of happiness seems to be inborn. Some babies are just easy to please, others find the world distressing. Optimists are happier (happy people would be optimistic, I guess). Happy people see themselves more positively than warranted, they overestimate the amount of personal control they have, and they are unrealistically optimistic about the future. In a way, you have to be a fool to be happy. You have to distort reality. Be a cockeyed optimist.

Being healthy, especially not having disabling and chronic illnesses, facilitates happiness, but having money does not (except for the very poor). That is true for individuals, but on a national level money does count. People in wealthy nations say they are happier than do persons in poor countries. Oddly, people who value money more highly than nonmaterialistic goals are less satisfied with their lives and with their standard of living. Values matter. Religious people are happier, or at least report more life satisfaction. Thank God for that.

Married people are happier. Older people are slightly more satisfied with life, even though there is a decline in positive affect with age. So you're not dancing in the street at 80, but you have more life satisfaction. Negative emotions don't change with age.

The effects of gender and education on happiness are unimpressive. No one group, it seems, has cornered the market on happiness. The researchers look at psychological processes like goal-setting and coping strategies. The flow, doing things that are challenging and worth doing for their own sake - running, mountain climbing, dancing, playing music - is another place they are looking. But if that were true, why aren't artists happy?

Too much candy at night balanced by too much caffeine during the day, sweetened by indulgences in homey summer delights - blueberry pie, ice cream, pizza, Carolina-

style barbecue potato chips - keep the tension well-stored in my shoulder and neck. The Sabbatical has not eradicated my trait anxiety, nor has it made a dent it the ways in which I handle it. But some things are new. For example, this summer I have some muscles under my fat.
My days begin with movement and a chat with a friend.
I smell like peaches and vanilla.
My life is more romantic.
And I think about work almost without regard to money!

Fall

1 September

A bite of a ripe peach, bought fresh from the orchard by the side of the road, is convincing evidence that God loves his creatures. Only a generous God would have invented peaches, with their sensual pleasures that can be enjoyed by young and old, and by every species! God must love us all, otherwise why would He take the trouble to make peaches?

2 September

Now that the summer is officially over, my Sabbatical has really, really begun. I feel more focused and invigorated, and less anxious and ambivalent about this phase. I have so many things I want to do, to read, to take care of in a more sophisticated way. There are things I want to let go of (reading the newspapers for an hour in the morning), and some I want to embrace (daily exercise) wholeheartedly.

3 September

Resolutions, good intentions...this time they died aborning. No one mourned them, not even me. I began my day with my newspaper ritual unchanged, and will no doubt end it without breaking a sweat. In some ways I live in a trance, continuing to do what I do, regardless of what I think I believe and intend.

Still dancing with resistance, I reorganized my closet this morning. It took about 15 minutes to do a job I hadn't been able to get to since we moved in a year ago. The clothes have been hanging the way the movers set them; I learned where to find them, and put them back where they "belonged." The system was awkward and made no sense, but the way things are is the way things are, which is so much more substantial than the way they might be. It seemed a daunting challenge to change the order. Revolution is a daunting challenge. I threw away a 12-year-old suit that's been out of style for 8, and left some ragged, shabby skirts because they haven't been replaced. Was I afraid of going naked? Am I too timid to risk facing the world for even a moment without a black wool skirt?

I went off in the afternoon to the Newseum (a news museum), not because I felt like it, but because it was one of the things I meant to do this summer. Not to do it was an affront to mindfulness, autonomy, and the gift of Sabbatical. Hearing myself say, "I've been meaning to go there, but I haven't gotten around to it yet," would be a confessing to a level of sloppiness out of control. I resist that chaos.

4 September

In my memory, the week of Erica's move to her own apartment will be filed under an icon of her in shorts and plastic sandals, talking about her 85 mosquito bites. 49 on one leg, she reported. Along with a headache, the excitement and stress of her move had a predictable effect. The same child who'd get sick anticipating birthday parties called in sick after she moved. But she did it.

Labor Day is a lightweight holiday snuck in under the door of somber September. The gift of a long weekend without family or ritual obligations. There's no special way one must feel on Labor Day, nothing to be observed. It is just the feast, if one wishes, of the last of summer's corn and tomatoes. Or a day at the mall.

Up here on the roof, in what I've come to think of as my personal meditation garden, the smell of basil wafts by. Three library books, time, and the silence of this wonderful retreat are bits of healing balm.

5 September

The noise level was high at the beach side restaurant in Cape May, NJ. Tables were full, set close together, and the diners were all having a good time enjoying the last part of the summer season. Two couples, down from Philadelphia, discussed their garden's dismal output this year. He had a booming voice, proclaiming, " You won't believe this, no zucchini, no eggplant. That's how bad it was." She told a story meant to be funny, about a cousin who broke a tooth while flossing. At the next table the conversation was softer, the smiles perhaps deeper and more conscious. He looked up at night sky and asked, "How do you know that God exists and that he cares for us?" "Because we're here," she answered simply, with only the least bit of explanation. "If there were no God, the universe would not exist. And one cares for that which she creates or nurtures."

That was the conclusion of my summer vacation.

6 September

Preparing for tomorrow evening's talk on the Psychology of Religion I notice how much more of the "spiritual" - a word I used to deride - understanding of religion makes sense to me. In that I'm right on developmental time; middle-aged, with greater respect for all that we don't control. I have long outgrown the arrogant youth's delusion of complete autonomy and control.

7 September

Resistance - Satan in three syllables.

8 September

I go through my day with underlying tension that reveals itself whenever I look for it. Today it manifested itself in wasteful impatience while I waited for my lunchtime felafel. I had no time limit. And lunch had merely been the excuse for leaving my office for another environment, for relaxing, and reading my book. I wasn't even hungry. But I couldn't just relax and read peacefully. I waited actively, checking my watch, thinking about whether I should go downstairs and inquire about why it was taking so long. Could a felafel really take more than 10 minutes?, I obsessed. In my mind I argued against even thinking about it. The blue painted walls around me were pleasing, the curtains fluttered prettily against the windows, stirred by the 75 degree autumn breeze. I had a seat by the window, with an espresso cup of Turkish coffee; I could enjoy reading here for half an hour without food. But I was anxious in minutes. The inner debate continued, squandering ten minutes - the entire universe of those ten minutes! I felt a sense of relief when the waiter brought my platter.

Relaxing, then, may be my challenge for the new season. Learning to live with what is, without needing to change it. Without rushing to the next imaginary goal, without moving anything, or wishing for anything. Being in each moment as it is. That is truly a challenge.

So I bought licorice tea and kava tea, herbal counterpoints to caffeine. One is never truly drug-free.

9 September

We brought a university student home from shul on Shabbat, who invited Elon out Saturday night, where he met Shoshana from San Francisco, who came over Sunday night to watch a movie. That's how connections work. During our now-traditional potluck seudah shlishit (the third Shabbat meal) with S. & L., they helped us place a painting in the evolving dining room. Their little daughter gave me a chance to regress, to pretend, and to laugh as I had not laughed all week. We put each other's shoes on, taking turns being Cinderella and the Prince. On Sunday, Jay and I shopped for a dining room rug and a freezerful of meat, preparations for the New Year. When we got home the H.s dropped by to chat, and to invite us to spend a few days with them in Ft. Lauderdale. Connections.

11 September

When I don't write, I don't remember. Three ordinary days have passed. The fact that they contained golden moments - of intimacy, friendship, intensity and worry, moments of irrational anger, public recognition and deep satisfaction - that I deem "ordinary," testifies to the richness of my life and my good fortune. I know that so much better when I write it down.

12 September

In 3 hours of conversation with G., I met a gentle man trying to save the world. He uses religion to bring peace, conflict resolution. He struggles to make peace with his own father's violence by healing it in the world. He would wish to be Gandhi, or Martin Luther King, who led their own people, but Jews do not follow his leadership, nor even acknowledge his goals. So he, the gentle man of peace, is angry at his own people for their failings.

13 September
ROSH HASHANAH

I recognized myself as a minority when I saw the quizzical expression on the salesman's face at Ben and Jerry's yesterday. I had ordered an ice cream cake that read "For a Sweet New Year."

Rosh Hashana. I think the message of the day is not the conventional explanation of justice, else why include the martyrology in the Yom Kippur service? Those stories tell of the good who suffered, not of people who got what they deserved. The challenge is how to live in the face of what life doles out. What will you make of your circumstances in the coming year? The message is "You don't know who will live and who die. You hope and pray for the best, but it really is not in your hands. Pay attention to what you can do; deal with your own actions, the meaning of your lives, the things that count that you can control. Hence, the vidui (confession).

15 September

Over this Rosh Hashana weekend *The Washington Post* reported an investigative study of children's deaths in the DC area. It seems that many more of them are homicides than had originally been reported. They also reported a story from Philadelphia in which a 19 year old Dominican immigrant, abandoned by the father of her 2 year old triplets, killed her babies and herself. Her tragedy reminded me of the prophet Jeremiah, who described the epitome of despair in his own time and forever in the image of a compassionate mother killing her child. Is killing one's child always an act of extreme despair, or just an extreme act? I learned in shul that the 100 blasts sounded on the shofar are modeled on the cries of Sisrah's mother in her grief upon hearing that her warrior son would not return from his battle with the Jews. We are so moved by the pain of a bereaved mother that the cries of the mother of our enemy became the template for the cries of our collective soul.

This remarkably relaxed Rosh Hashanah passed pleasantly. With ten people around our table each day, we welcomed the new year with warmth, friendship, and satisfaction. I will work on my issues, considering more often the possibility that I could be wrong. Other people will work on theirs.

16 September

We enjoyed two elegant, sumptuous Rosh Hashanah evening meals here in our little corner of Foggy Bottom. Lunch at home was a young crowd, 6 twentysomethings and us. The last lunch was just the "family," at L's. It doesn't get better than this. In shul and out, I tried to introspect, and the conclusion I came to for this coming year is "lighten up!" That has meaning for me in terms of meditation, in terms of family relations, and in terms of my interminable sense of redefining myself. Lighten up - - I took all my political books back to the library (*How Clinton Betrayed America; The Lexus and the Olive Tree*), and all my good, but terribly serious ones (*The Ascent of Man* —maybe another time). I wandered the bookshelves and here's what I picked on

Tishrei 3, Tzom Gedalia: *Zen Mind, Beginner's Mind*, by Shunryu Suzuki, and *All of One Peace* (a good intention, poorly executed by Coleman McCarthy). Blessings of Peace to all in the New Year.

From *Zen Mind*: "These forms are not a means of obtaining the right state of mind. To take this posture itself is the purpose of our practice. When you have this posture, you have the right state of mind, so there is no need to try to attain some special state. When you try to attain something, your mind starts to wander about somewhere else. When you do not try to attain anything, you have your own body and mind right here."

Or, to put it another way, "lighten up!"

17 September

Walks along the Potomac nourish an image I keep returning to: a river of compassion. I sail on it, swim in it. It flows through me toward others. It is a soothing, musical image of comfort and reassurance that bears my name, Ruchama.

19 September

Some people's drug is activity. "As long as I keep busy I'm all right," they say. Anxiety rushes in to any spaces unfilled by "busy." Others eat, worry, take lovers, gossip. It is no less a drug if the motivation is more positive, i.e., the pursuit of pleasure rather than the avoidance of discomfort.

Approach or avoidance, all intrinsic actions function much as drugs do: the recreational user seeks pleasure, the addict uses to avoid pain. All these drugs differ only in their harmfulness, and the degree to which they limit the user's freedom (how hard it would be for them to choose not to use that drug, a measure of the strength of attachment). The pursuit of pleasure takes many forms, not all of them obvious. The lover in pursuit of the beloved, the artist who "must" paint, the compulsion to "follow one's bliss" share the same blindness, though we admire them. Human actions that don't fit the drug model are those committed to because of belief in a principle. Religious observance, or any other-based system of discipline may promise joy, enlightenment or holiness as the long-term payoff, but the practitioner exercises because of her commitment, her faith.

Submission to a Higher Power is the only alternative to a life of drugs, just as they say in AA.

20 September

This week a friend and a patient both complained about their loneliness, their isolation. It resonated in me when I reflect on how few people I talk to besides Jay. Who would I call just because I felt like talking? I asked another patient what she did for fun, and heard her describe how fun occasions became work (an investment club, a writer's group). All of this Washington pathology, where neighborly chats have a scheduled time and a task to produce, and fun sounds like a trick question. What makes you laugh?, I explained, what do you look forward to eagerly? What do you like to do just for itself, not for its product? What, indeed?

21 September

A.L. stopped by today, bringing the particular pleasure of old, good friendship. We drank a glass of wine, and I accompanied her to the airport where I had a chance to see her anxiety at work. It was like finally meeting a monstrous relative whose stories your friend has been telling for years. Upon meeting them in the flesh they do, in fact, seem unpleasant, but almost conventional in their familiarity.

"We have so many blessings," Val said at lunch the other day. The challenge is to keep them in focus when clouds of irritation, depression and problems fog the lens.

22 September

I have to smile at the anxiety with which I anticipate my meeting with my editor. I question my motives, my choices. Why did I leave out that important issue of people specializing in their defects? What sentimental slop I included! Judgment is indeed feared. Hence Yom Kippur.

24 September

How odd it is that today, just after Yom Kippur, my e-mail inbox is filled with discussions of God's ways in punishment and rewards, his role in good and evil. And they couldn't have come from more different sources! The Disaster Mental Health listserv is discussing how to help the teenage survivors of the Ft. Worth killings (another madman with an automatic weapon - this one selected a teen prayer service at a Baptist church in Texas.) who ask, agonizing, how God could let this happen. The other is the adoption listserv which is having a lively discussion about the appropriateness of some adoptive parents feeling that God arranged for their child to come to them. Did God therefore also see fit to arrange for the *tzoris* (troubles) that preceded the placement? ask some others. There is passion in the discussion.

What is the traditional answer to why Abraham didn't argue with God about the binding of Isaac the way he did when Sodom was slated for destruction? Was it because it wasn't positioned as punishment, so there could be no appeal to justice? Was it because Abraham understood that taking Isaac to the altar didn't necessarily mean his death - perhaps Abraham lived in the moment, and heard the exact words God said without getting distracted by their implication or his fear of their implication? I must find out before I yield to the temptation of the psychological explanation of Abraham's murderous inclinations toward his sons, his willingness to participate in their destruction. Abe didn't argue with God about the wisdom of following Sarah's suggestion and banishing Ishmael to the desert. Why would God say, "Go on, send Ishmael out to his death like Sarah said", and then intervene to save the boy? Wouldn't it have been simpler and more instructive to advise Abraham to banish him in a way that preserved the boy's life and his dignity? In a way that wasn't designed to engender Ishmael's eternal anger toward the father who tried to kill him, and the son for whose benefit he was to be sacrificed?

25 September

Two old patients returned yesterday, and I was struck anew by how much of the pain we experience we cause ourselves. Not because we want to, of course, just because of our hidden beliefs and fears, most of which are fantasies, and because of our attachments to our wishes and desires. It's not much of an insight for someone who's been a shrink since 1974, but it struck me again yesterday. In the freshness of the day after Yom Kippur, I felt sympathy for us poor mortals, so limited in the reach of our understanding. (I still don't really "get" how space can be curved, or what the space-time continuum really is. And I bet the mind is a lot harder to know than simple relativity!) Still, both patients - both mid-life women - were also experiencing growing pains. The first regretted the limitations she had placed on her life; living life small and controlled had robbed her of passion. My job with her was that of a midwife - to help the repressed, inhibited parts of herself emerge safely. The second patient had confronted the fragility of life, rather obliquely - she had been laid off from a job she enjoyed and despite finding another equally good position, she was feeling inexplicably anxious and not happy. Change you do not ask for, or expect, when it happens at 50, can carry a larger message. Her friend's father has Pick's Disease - that ugly imitation of Alzheimer's - and he is the same age as my patient's husband.

Meanwhile, last month's earthquake in Turkey has been followed by another big one in Taiwan. And the people of East Timor have either been hacked to death or are homeless refugees.

26 September

I took an old-fashioned approach to blowing away the light gray of my mood. Better than a new hat, I bought a ridiculously overpriced cologne that smells like chocolate! Amour de Cacao is the French name (with a French price) for a chocolate-chip-cookie-smelling spray that makes my gastric juices flow. It smells good enough to eat! The very idea of it makes me giggle, sniffing myself makes me smile. It's worth every penny.

28 September

This is a moment of in-between. Only when I stop to notice it, instead of fleeing from it - to putter or read or make a cup of coffee - only now can I notice that it is a moment for itself, not just in-between. I am waiting for Jim Lieberman to call back to tell me it's okay to post his fine essay, "Why Oedipus Loved His Father", on the *ASI* website. I'm waiting for a reviewer to comment on an article. I'm waiting for the children to navigate their current hurdles and land safely, on the right path.

The Sabbatical mode is sinking in. I can recognize my Mom's twice-daily phone calls as work, as I do my calls to her caregivers and to others about her financial issues. As a job I do not resent them. This week I went to the gym at 9 AM - twice. It felt different to be there during "work" time instead of before or after. I was there, working out was what I was doing, instead of pushing it in, stealing time from something else, or feeling tired and ambivalent. I spent the greatest part of one day editing the galleys for Issue 3. I didn't have to do it in the evening, or feel the pull of 50 uncompleted tasks screaming from their piles for my attention. "Working" on projects that matter without regard for the money they make is satisfying, and it is work, but it is work you can't complain about, since it is autonomously chosen and voluntarily engaged in. I feel so fortunate to have this experience.

29 September

I often confound understanding with doing. Once I know something, I lose interest in it. In that respect I haven't changed much since I baked a chocolate cake when I was 10. It looked, smelled and tasted like a chocolate cake. I had "gotten the idea" about baking, so what would be the point of doing it again?

Of all experiences, the most satisfying to me are understanding and making contact. Understanding, knowing, is a kind of contact; it's making contact on a particular dimension. Love is contact; it is "knowing" on another dimension. The person happily in love feels uniquely understood by the beloved. On our way home from a pleasant dinner party with people I like, I reflected what was lacking in that form of social gathering. It doesn't permit me to make real contact with people. I leave knowing no one any better than I did before. That is why, I suppose, it is called "entertaining." Like television, it passes the time pleasantly enough, but nothing sticks to the ribs. It is mere diversion. It feels like a waste of time.

30 September

After *Turbulent Souls*, and *The Color of Water*, I've begun reading Aharon Applefeld's *Conversion*. *The Washington Post* calls it a fable of prewar Austria. I am fascinated by the phenomenon of conversion, as the personification of the search for spiritual or religious fit. People change themselves, or find themselves. They seek solace, acceptance, connection. They want an open phone line instead of a busy signal. They want a reflection of what is most beautiful and precious in themselves, the best they can imagine. They want to reflect God, to embrace Him, to know Him. There isn't anything a human being won't do when she finds that.

With so many people searching, and so many open paths already trodden, why is there still so much ugliness in the world?

Thomas Merton

By coincidence (itself a controversial concept), the volume of Merton's diaries on the West End library's shelf was the journal of his 50th year. Merton (1915-1968) spent 27 years in a Trappist monastery, the most ascetic Catholic monastic order. His contemplative life seemed to impel him far beyond the monastery walls, as a political activist for peace and civil rights and as a prolific writer. He was not your standard monk. Later in life he became interested in Asian religions, particularly Zen Buddhism. Since his good friends included both Suzuki and Abraham Joshua Heschel, perhaps it's not so odd that I, too, feel I can relate to him. Merton reminded me of myself; his diaries are the inner life of a person like all of us, annoyed, irritable, struggling with health problems and his own limitations. Having trouble managing the flow of demands on his time, obsessing about his physical surroundings, commenting on the weather. The breadth of his scholarship and literary and religious connections were impressive, but no more so than his ordinary humanity. Take, for example, page 19, which reminded me of my own geographic ambivalence:

"To accept my life in this context. Not to try to force this place into some arbitrary meaning or pattern. It is just that I am now in Louisville and last night I was under those trees, and I do not have to make sense out of it, still less to force it to "make sense" which would, in fact be to insist on an illusion."

October

1 October

I slept fitfully my second night as a houseguest. Twice, I awakened from dreams involving getting rid of trash. In the first I was looking for the incinerator which I had somehow misplaced in my own building. The second dream involved cleaning out a large, old-fashioned standing ashtray. Convinced that my unconscious was trying to tell me something important, I went back to sleep willing myself to dream another, clarifying message. Naturally, I drew a blank. Later in the day I wondered whether my sleeping mind was merely reacting to visual overstimulation. My dreams may have been housekeeping wish-fulfillment, trying to clean up the clutter of our Victorian environment. Our hosts live with so much stuff! Cabinets full of knickknacks. Candles, candelabras and potpourri on every counter. Framed family photographs layers-deep on every table top. Collections of vases, flea market antiques, Old hotel memorabilia. Patterned wallpaper on every wall, vases and lacy curtains, and rooms overstuffed with furniture. I came home thinking about giving away every bit of useless clothing in my closet.

Visits with old friends or family are invitations to gossip. Gossip is such a delicious temptation. It's almost sexual in its seductiveness. Like illicit sex, it appears to draw people close. It has voyeuristic elements - you look deep into another person's private life, observe, analyze, judge, and become passionate about their behavior. It feels intimate and exciting. But like hurried sex in a cheap motel, gossip also feels sordid, leaving one cheapened and sullied. In a moment of passion, you stoop to your baser instincts. Encouraged and excited by your partner, you abandon inhibition, and let go. When it is over he - and you - know what you are capable of, and you're both disappointed. You can't pretend it never happened. The embrace of gossip evokes pleasure and release - you can't really stop in the middle unless interrupted, and it is so much fun while it lasts! Still, there are some regrets the next morning. Something's been lost in the transaction, and nothing gained.

2 October

About 18 years ago I stopped eating meat. That is, except for my annual trip to NY, when I'd indulge in a triple-decker pastrami combo sandwich at my favorite deli. Besides enjoying both the nostalgia and the dish, I liked demonstrating that my vegetarianism was a preference, not a religion. I preferred to live my life without killing animals, but I didn't want to be fanatic about it. Mine was a gentle, cerebral vegetarianism, not a moral judgment. I felt fine about buying and preparing meat for others. But last night I glanced at the brisket our host served, and I felt disgusted. It was a corpse lying there, tender and perfectly cooked. Sauce, gravy, and slicing couldn't hide the brisket's resemblance to the squirrel carcass we had watched a cat carry proudly into the yard. For Kitty, that squirrel was a prime cut of meat, a delicacy to be properly savored. She trotted by us, head held high, a fastidious housewife favored by her butcher.

My first vegetarian impulse came at age 8, when I saw a whole tongue, unsliced, on a platter in the kitchen. Oh, my God, we were going to eat someone's tongue! Like most city children, I hadn't made the connection between meat and the animal it had once been. Once that connection was made, I refused even to think about tongue, let alone eat it, for the next 10 years. But at 18, I was far too mature to be bothered by such childish sensitivities. Many children are revolted by the idea of eating meat ("you mean we're eating Bambi!!"), but most get used to it, the way they get used to smoking cigarettes, drinking liquor, the bitter taste of black coffee, the fecal smell of cigars. Innocents react to many things with revulsion - which is followed quickly by collusion. We are so eager to acquire taste and be sophisticated, that we beg to be initiated into the darker pleasures. Darkness seduces, and we follow it into the night.

7 October

Perhaps the reason God created Man, or the reason he entered into a Covenant, is that only in a relationship is God greater than One. In a relationship the whole is greater than the sum of its parts. If one part of the couple is infinite, the other can't add to Him, but He is nevertheless enlarged because of the relationship. The relationship adds another dimension. God can only be a partner when he is in a relationship. The Yom Kippur liturgy asks for God's compassion - as a father to his sons, a master to his servants, a lover to his beloved, a shepherd to his sheep, a creator to his creations - all appeal to the relationship. Without us He is still One, still perfect, but not in a relationship. If this can be said about the Infinite without sounding disrespectful, God would be diminished without us; He'd be perfectly self-sufficient, of course, and perhaps not even lonely, but He would not be engaged. The only thing The One "lacks" is the other.

And that's why He wants us to be his holy nation. The holy nation is separated, not just from other nations, but from God himself. Man wants to merge with God, to please him and be safe. One way to cull favor is to be obedient, to submit your will to His. But other nations excel in submission. We've had trouble with that from the beginning. Our charge isn't blind obedience for its own sake. Our charge is to follow His directions in order to become holy. When we are merely submissive we are like the simpering, self-denying date who drives you crazy with her desire to please: "I don't mind." "Whatever you want to see is fine." "Sure, whatever you like." That's not us. We are supposed to stand upright through His laws, to dignify ourselves through the tradition. That's how we can develop the kind of personality (peoplehood) that is differentiated enough to be a worthwhile partner, a significant other.

8 October

I know how a squirrel must feel. Yesterday was a crisp fall day, and, and like a squirrel driven to gather nuts, I needed to fill a shopping cart. Our freezer had been filled the day before, to my great satisfaction, when we got a delivery of meat and kosher items. We neglected to mention what size we wanted in some items, so we ended up with too much — baba ganush and veggie chopped liver in the super size, six gallons of grape juice, two lbs of marshmallow fluff are really more than we need. But who cares—there's home delivery! Since we really didn't need much, I performed the weekly grocery shopping at Rodman's, where food selection retains some of the adventure that it must have had for hunter-gatherers long ago. Rodman's is a drugstore that grew with no apparent plan; its inventory is unpredictable. Browsing Rodman's is an exercise in discovery. My haul included coconut milk, an electric broom and - what a find!- kosher candy-style calcium supplements. Now I can eat chocolate for breakfast while preventing osteoporosis!

I shopped the way autumn flirts with Washington. It engages the city in motion like lovers' foreplay. A small move forward, then coy retreat. In early October a cool day will be followed by several spring-like wonders. The leaves are still mostly green, with only hints of brown and red and orange. Progress toward winter is so gentle here, it can almost go unnoticed. Autumn moves slowly, protectively, as if to reassure the city that although winter is coming, it won't be too harsh or stay too long. October announces that one needn't be afraid of the future.

I celebrated fall, bringing mums and gourds and baby pumpkins home, and CDs of Italian Baroque music, "world" guitar music, and, for Jay, something called Sephardi spiritual chants.

Or perhaps the chants were not really for Jay. They may end up in my office, next to the Tibetan chants. I am reading a book about life in a Benedictine monastery in North Dakota (*The View from a Monastery*, by Brother Benet Tvedten), and it occurred to me that my office serves me as a kind of monastery. It's white and wood and uncluttered. Candles and music create a space of tranquility and focus. I have a routine that with only a little attention could become a discipline. It is quiet much of the time in my office, and in the quiet, I contemplate, like monks do. Or perhaps I am less like a monk, who lives communally, and more like a hermit. While I'm there, I don't see many people besides patients. Nobody ever drops by unexpectedly, nor would that be welcome, the way it would be at home. I am quite fond of my little space. I look forward to my solitude there, solitude whose value resides in its balance with the rest of my life.

10 October

A sympathetic character in the movie *Waking Ned Devine* lied about her son's paternity. The prevailing orthodoxy in the field of adoption is that it is vital to know that you were adopted, and very healthy to know about your biological parents. I know three people who don't know they're adopted. And if I know of three, how many are there that I don't know about? It's commonly accepted that each of us knows many more gay people than the ones that are "out." If 20% of married women have had affairs, how many have become pregnant? It's been estimated that 10% of us are not the offspring of the men we call Dad.

A case of babies switched at birth came to light recently because of a paternity suit. DNA testing determined that the child was neither parent's biological offspring. Had money not been an issue, triggering the paternity suit, neither child would ever have suspected they were biologically unrelated to their families. Each child's idiosyncrasies and differences from her parents and sibs would perhaps have been noticed and explained...as they are with all of us. I always felt profoundly different from my parents and sister. In retrospect, that feeling was part of my development as an individual, and part "objectively" true. I was different, despite biological bonds. I wonder how many undiscovered switches happen in hospitals?

But that is a different topic. Back to this one, there is good reason to believe that a fair minority of us are unrelated to at least one of our parents. Those folks apparently live quite well without knowing about it. Does that challenge the prevailing, politically correct adoption orthodoxy?

12 October

The hallway table says fall. It says everything about the season. On the right are a lulav in a vase, the esrog nestled in its silver box. Today their job is over, but their dignity remains. Balancing on the left are a basket of gourds and a vase with fragrant lilies. The gourds in the basket look ripe. They are bright orange and green, round and full; ready, even eager to feed you. Their warm colors say that they want to satisfy. They appear to be filled not just with nourishment, but with compassion.

White lilies pose gracefully against the dark green wall. Their petals seem to reach up in a silent dance of gratitude. Their fragrance, like frankincense and myrrh, rises and spreads the message.

13 October

"Too many covers," I thought when I awoke at 7, my back and chest clammy in a familiar way that reminded me of our children waking up in their cribs after a deep, long nap. I turned over for another hour of sleep and awoke smiling from a dream that featured "ice age perfume"! The unconscious mind solves problems with a sense of humor.

14 October

I hopped a cab to meet Elon for lunch today. The cabbie was listening to tapes of the psalms. We rode in silence listening to Psalm 23... the Hebrew echoing in my mind as the everyday American translation was read by a warm baritone. There are so many ways to sanctify the moment.

October 15

I feel like canceling my subscription to *Jerusalem Report* for a while, and reading the *New Yorker* instead. Filled with cartoons, urbane humor, drollery and ads for expensively frivolous items, the *New Yorker* exudes a sense of security, prosperity, and the kind of easygoing, assumed well-being that allows you to laugh at yourself. Probably some of its readers will respond to its ads and actually buy the Freudian Slippers, Nantucket mug, and 18 flavors of pecans. Those are not people worried about being overrun at any moment by virulent mobs of Jew-hating Arabs. I didn't notice an ad for designer gas masks.

18 October

I want to be sure to remember that golden afternoon in a playground in Brooklyn. Last Sunday was one of those rare, perfect New York City autumn days, when the sun is warm, and the leaves have turned to gold, with enough of them on the ground to soften the hard lines of an urban playground. The playground was full of children playing together like an ad for American diversity. Asian and Hispanic, Russian and Chassidic, small groups of children each with an attentive - but not necessarily English-speaking - adult nearby. The children were polite, waiting their turns, shouting "excuse me!" when a distracted little one came too close to the swirling merry-go-round. The adults talked to one another, just enough to maintain the atmosphere of cordial good humor and trust. "May I help you?" chirped a young Chinese mother at me, holding out her camera. She was asking me to take a photograph of her little family, with a charming inversion of word order. A mother from Canton was studying English phrases to be able to answer the phone in the factory where she worked. No one in her workplace can speak English. Her kids, 3 and 6 years old, of course, do. A young Hispanic man was there with his nephew, a gentle boy of 8. The uncle, 23, was bossy and hovering, but open and likable as he explained his family life to me. And I? I sat next to my old mother, enjoying the breeze and the children. We could share this moment as two adults. She was quiet, but engaged. It was the best 40 minutes of our day. To amuse us both I got on a swing, my legs pumping high, and waved to her. She smiled and waved back. When I returned, laughing at my childish fun, she said, "Why shouldn't you swing? You're young." I laughed, "I'm big enough to push myself on the swings now, Ma. You don't have to push me anymore."

When it was time to go I unlocked the brakes of her wheelchair and pushed it down the street.

21 October

The blind woman was upset. She couldn't shake her fury against a fellow committee member. We had all been gathered to advise the Adoption Institute on their forthcoming Ethics Conference when one asked, "what will we say to the adult adoptee who comes to us in the future complaining about having been placed with disabled parents - that we had no choice because of ADA (Americans with Disabilities Act)?" Her words, like those special bullets that tear up their victim's insides, struck their mark between two sightless eyes.

Their impact made no sound. And the damage that resulted was invisible to everyone, except the blind woman.

22 October

Resistance is the most loyal companion. It is right beside me, urging me to catch up with my files, and make unnecessary phone calls. Its motive is clear: to make sure I procrastinate and become as alienated as possible from writing my editorial. One of its tools is fear of public judgment: I might express myself clumsily. Perhaps I don't have enough to say. People will criticize and think less of me....I will expose the thin nature of my "expertise" in adoption. D. noted that I am rare among gerontologists; most people go into aging late in their career, I have left it.

With only an hour left until my next appointment, I think I'll put off my writing for another day. Resistance, my little buddy, is very persuasive.

26 October

I wouldn't mind if I die. I'm not suicidal at all; I take a daily vitamin and even think about exercise.

Maybe what I mean by dying is what Thomas Merton wrote in his diary on Jan 25, 1965:

"My intention is, in fact, simply to 'die' to the past somehow. To take my 50th birthday as a turning point and to live more abandoned to God's will, less concerned with projects and initiatives (which have, however, perhaps also been His will). More detached from work and events, more solitary. To be one of those who entirely practice contemplation simply in order to follow God. And who am I anyway?"

Two weeks later Merton was so upset about having been refused permission to travel to an ecumenical meeting that he couldn't sleep. He felt misjudged, misunderstood, held captive by his vow of obedience to the prejudice of smaller men. He is cheered by his mail, his projects. He says:

"It is good to be part of all that too! Alas! Vanity. But that is the thing about solitude. To realize how desperately we depend on the 'existence' that recognition gives us, and how hopeless we are without it until God gives us feet to stand alone on. I have those feet sometimes, but once again, let me realize that there is no absolute 'standing alone' ..."

I've experienced the grace. I have the solitude and the projects. And I surely have the ambivalence!

I seem always to find something in Merton's diaries. A gem

mixed into the middle of theological ideas that I cannot accept. In the midst of musing about martyrdom as the pinnacle of a believer's life (an idea that doesn't work for me at all), he comments on the following, which struck him while preparing a sermon ("which", he noted without further comment, "people seemed to like yesterday"):

> "...the thought took a deep hold on me that what matters in our life is not abstract ideals but profound love and surrender..."

Merton's words reminded me of my aunt's husband's advice about how old people can stay young: "Accept everything with love."

Merton feels he has been called to his life. My old friend C. believes that everyone has a particular, unique mission. She has always believed that. I do not. I never knew what to do with that idea. Can it be that people seek their mission and never find it? Like their one true love? What a tragedy! Perhaps people seek it and miss living their lives while they're on the lookout for it. Maybe the mission is to live what is, because no one else has the opportunity to live your particular life. So everyone's calling is to be enlightened; to live life consciously in the moment. See what I mean by not knowing what to do with the idea? Is everyone called, but most of us are deaf? The image of people living their lives asleep, unconscious, is found in all traditions whose aim is to awaken them to the Truth. What if we don't like what our mission is supposed to be? (Then change it. It's still your mission.) What if we want to choose something else? (Just wait. Something else will be here.) What if your one true love is an ax murderer, a philanderer, and a no-good louse? "B'shert" means predestined. What if you have been predestined for misery? K. said accept everything with love (a striking directive from someone in the Yeshiva world). So would Merton and Ram Surya Das and probably Suzuki. Still, somehow these ideas of mission, b'shert and calling seem to substitute one's own judgment ("it feels so right. We were meant for each other") for His.

29 October

Religiously speaking, the world is like a locked room with a picture window. When the window is dirty or fogged with the breath of humanity, all its inhabitants can know is what is in the room. When the window is clean, those inside can look out to the larger space beyond.

Cultures develop methods, styles, rules, and disciplines along with detailed beliefs about the best and proper ways to wash the window, to keep it clean in order to peer outside. Sometimes the detailed rituals - the correct position, the social rotation, the rules defining who what when where and how the window is washed become so important in themselves that the room's residents forget all about looking out through it! They become a nation of traditional window-washers, oblivious to the vista outside. But as long as window-washing continues, there is a chance that someone will look out. Maybe that's what it means to be a "light unto the nations". We are supposed to be a nation of window-washers, living lives that let the outside shine through!

In other cultures the windows remain dirty, devalued or ignored in favor of action inside the room. When the window is dirty enough and there is no window-washing tradition, the culture forgets that there is a window at all. Then what's in the room is all there is. And if you don't believe there is a window, you never look for one. Occasionally, an individual will try looking out. He may try stepping on tiptoe and craning his neck to find a clear spot, even without the support of window washers. The few who report what they see are called prophets.

Mahanabrata Brahmachari, a Hindu scholar, died yesterday at the age of 95. His obituary noted that he had introduced Thomas Merton to St. Augustine. I feel like Merton is introducing me to my own spirituality, as he said of the lesson Brahmachari's life taught: "that one can and must entrust himself to a higher and unseen Wisdom, and that if one can relax his frantic hold on the illusory securities of everyday material existence and abandon himself peacefully to a Supreme Will, he will himself find freedom and peace in that Will."

I need to learn that lesson.

November

3 November

Reading *The Artist's Way* reminds me that I have lived my life creatively. When I told him about *Adoption Quarterly*, my former boss Bill responded, admiringly, "you've always been able to find your own niche."

It was creative to go to Copenhagen to work for Sarnoff, to wrest a degree from Lund, to help invent gerontology. Making a lucrative consulting practice out of one small idea, taking the family to Eilat, starting an academic journal, taking a sabbatical, turning my observations in the Gulf War into travel with the Red Cross....what I normally bemoan as frivolous dilettantism can just as well be called creativity. I took my interest in the psychology of religion and turned it into a four- week course. That is at least as creative as taking an interest in flowers and turning it into a painting.

4 November

The voices that urge me to look for a job, a bigger project, a challenge are still there, but now I give them amused notice. They are the voices of narcissism, the voices of anxiety. They believe that if one does something big enough, important enough, it justifies living. Or it defies death. They chime an old chorus, one that is hard to ignore completely, but is not worth serious critical review. A friend's friend asked me whether this year is preparation for retirement, and I answered, "maybe." I will not force the issue.

Some days I imagine creating the Humor Institute, an organization with no seriousness at all, that promotes laughter, whose mission statement is: Lighten up!!!

6 November

"I'm so proud of having made that gravlax", I told everyone who would listen. It's an odd dish, marinated, not cooked, that needs attention at regular intervals over 48 hours. What I was really proud of was that serving gravlax as an appetizer meant I had thought about Shabbat on Wednesday. Thinking ahead to Shabbat on Wednesday is a change, something I had never been able to do in the past. Not just because life used to be less predictable and more crisis-ridden. Thinking about Shabbat on Wednesday elevates Shabbat from a mere day (with particular requirements) to an event. Shabbat as an event becomes organized to create an ambience, with content, context, feel and satisfaction. This past week, our lunch table, pretty with new china and old silver - and the unusual gravlax - had the early 20's set at one end (I insensitively sat them at the table extension, certain that they would prefer to be cozily together. Instead each one of the four instantly commented about the "kiddie table." I won't make that mistake again!), a thirtyish couple in the middle, and a late middle-aged couple with their young child at the end. I felt the evolving elder role as a cocoon-eating insect might her emerging butterfly self. Who did they see when they watched me go into the kitchen for the next course? What did they hear when I related how we had to have our arms twisted to finally pick out a silver pattern before we got married? "It was the sixties," Jay said by way of explanation, to an audience for whom the sixties might as well have been the Roaring Twenties. "We were very young and not into the trappings of marriage," I explained to polite, blank faces. "You were young?", they might be thinking. "You were getting married!?" It seems we have been married forever. They only see fat cats, in an apartment unimaginably big, on the far side of a gulf they do not imagine themselves ever crossing.

11 November

It's Veteran's Day. In sympathy, it seemed, a tree in Georgetown bled graceful yellow leaves all over N Street. The sky held tight to its stoic gray, permitting itself only the brief relief of a drizzle, a hint of tears.

12 November

I love my life when I write it. The act of writing turns diffuse light - the mundane life, the twinkling moments of recognition - into a clear beam. Focus, focus, focus...and ordinary daylight becomes a brilliant laser. They're both the same, except for the focus.

Happiness

Sometimes it seems that people's feeling-tones have a "set-point", a pattern of mixed happiness and sadness, anxiety and calm that is their personal profile into which they fit their life's events. Big events like a death, loss of a job or falling in love will color the pattern for a while, and might even set a path, but then the pattern will return to its normal range, and life will be used to explain it. If you are awake, you know that what happens on shore doesn't cause the tides to move, and the movement of the tides influences life only in subtle, but still unmeasured ways.

16 November

Seventy people burned to death in the crash of a commuter train at Paddington station in London.

Modern man is as vulnerable to random tragedy as his primitive ancestor: in one week there was an earthquake in Oaxaca, Mexico, and a nuclear reactor accident in Tokyo, Japan. And why should our continuing vulnerability even be worth mentioning? Where do we get the arrogance to even consider that we may have evolved to protect ourselves against tragedy? We certainly have not evolved beyond the evil we inflict on our own species! Chaos, anarchy, aggression, and violence are our intimates, even as they were to our less "civilized" ancestors. We die in a commuter train fireball, wearing a suit and tie, worrying about our stock portfolio, or we die under a pile of rocks - our home - shaken loose by a nudge of tectonic plates, or we die at the hand of our neighbor. Better to die in bed, at the right time, having said a loving goodbye to our children and grandchildren, and our friends of course, but die we must. We are all the dead of the future - a sobering thought. I will die, but probably not today. So will you. When I contemplate that in the future you will be dead I feel compassion toward you, as toward anyone with a terminal condition. I feel like lingering with you, holding your hand and smoothing your hair. My eyes tear just thinking that you -and I- will lose one another one day. How could I ever be unkind or angry at someone who will die?

The future-dead evoke sympathy. We are repelled by them, too, because we don't want to share in their fate. Nevertheless, we must. Everyone reading this will die. Their babies, not yet conceived, will die. Life is just a little interlude between eternities of non-living. Get used to it... and have a nice day.

17 November

Today I saw a patient who described the dress she was fixing for her shroud. She planned to replace the silver belt buckle with one that had some black on it to pick up the black in the onyx necklace she'd wear. A friend had been sent to buy her a new pair of white cotton panties. Her slip and stockings were prepared. "Is there anything else we need to talk about?" she asked. She does not want to die, she had hoped to live longer, but the past year has been so hard, and she is so weak and tired. She looks forward to rest, to peace. Such a dying is sobering to watch, and a little sad - as all partings are sad - but not frightening or depressing. Driving home in the rain I missed my exit, feeling the familiar anxiety rise as I muttered curses at the Virginia highway signage department. Then I caught myself, and smiled. In the face of death, most distress - boiled down to its essential narcissistic rage at Life daring to deviate from one's wishes - seems ludicrous.

18 November

I went to an alternative service last Shabbat. "Fabrengen" is the name of an egalitarian minyan, a havurah, one of the first of its kind founded in the late 1960s. Just two blocks from home, it took time travel to get there. Women in clogs, large kippot and talitot. I've never gotten used to the use of masculine religious symbols by women. Who wants to look like junior men? But a mother and daughter led part of the service, and other parts were led by people sitting around the room, which resulted in a lovely feeling of inclusion. They only chanted a third of the Torah portion, but the entire portion was read in English by passing the book around. The instructive sermon was given by the daughter of the bride whose "aufruf" (Shabbat celebration honoring an upcoming marriage) was being celebrated. The speaker and her four sibs were raised at Fabrangen, and they are actively Jewish. The daughter who chanted the Torah portion wore a hat and is a member of an Orthodox synagogue. So, who knows? There was more apparent Kavanah (sincerity, intention), more enthusiasm, pleasure, and involvement in prayer than I am accustomed to seeing in Orthodox synagogues. The community knows one another. They participate, they connect, they are in touch. It takes work to be part of this group, where every decision is discussed, every element considered. But it is a group, there is something to be part of. There is something attractive there: an openness, a lack of pretense and formality that is so alienating in more conventional religious environments. Perhaps it is a lack of judgementalism, or perhaps not. It is a commitment to connection above all. But I can't relate to the Reconstructionist siddur. Kathleen Norris noted in *Cloister Walk* that modernizers of the liturgy lose the depths of metaphor when they trade it in for politically correct prose. They don't get it. That's how I feel about various versions of Conservative, Reform and Reconstructionist siddurim. What's wrong with being a Chosen people, happy to be who you are, glad you weren't born anywhere else? If you're happy to be married to your spouse, and glad he chose you, do you need to rush in to say other people were chosen to be married by fine men, too? Do you need to worry that you sound superior (my man is the best! He chose me, not you!)? It is neither exclusivist nor elitist to be glad one is who and where one is.

19 November

Part of illusion in the search for the good life, or in philosophy or religion, is the idea that if you find the right answer then you keep it. The message in recommending a "way" (Halacha means the path) is the recognition that your ship is always battered by the waves, or there is no ship, only waves - and still you keep going in the "way," on the path, guided by the light of the moon. Only a fool would ask the ocean to be still, or believe there was no land anywhere because the earth is round and all he can see is water.

20 November

I dressed in front of the TV this morning. The *Leeza* show featured serial killers, exploiting the sorrow of parents of murdered children. The kitchen radio dully explained changes in Special Education in the District. Moving from one room to the other made me feel surrounded by insanity; America can neither educate its children nor keep them alive. Killings are more interesting. Below the fold in today's newspaper is part two of a feature about 2 teenage murderers, brothers, who grew up here in D.C. I put aside the morning paper to read Applefeld. Somehow the experiences of an Austrian bureaucrat four generations ago are more compelling to me than news of my contemporaries. The past can be studied, savored, reviewed, and analyzed. But current events are a tornado; chaos and debris move with great force in an entirely unpredictable course. Those who come later examine the path of destruction.

22 November

Adam Phillips' book, *On Kissing, Tickling and Being Bored* notes "...boredom is akin to free-floating attention...the capacity to be bored can be a developmental achievement for the child." Boredom is a kind of depression, an emptiness of attention rather than of affect. When I don't want to do anything, I just want to "relax." To relax, i.e., to quiet that uncomfortable edge of energy that sizzles without direction. Unconnected attention is boredom; an unpleasant state that demands to be changed.

23 November

The radio is on as I wait for the internet to come up with the latest weather report. (It feels like snow - should we shop early for the upcoming long holiday weekend?) While I wait, I read one of my new library books, *The Presence of Absence: on prayers and an epiphany* by Doris Grumbach. She describes her private journey inward. Solitude and silence enabled her to pray, when 50 years of faithful church attendance did not. I am comfortable receiving three simultaneous sources of input, one which extols quietude. But the irony does not escape me. I am amused.

25 November

About an hour ago I realized that I was in heaven.

Regardless of what imagery or metaphors are used to express it, Paradise is a concept made up of circumstances so pleasing, one can imagine enjoying them eternally, without surfeit and without change. It's a tough concept, given our human penchant for boredom, our need for novelty, divine discontent, curiosity. It is hard for me to imagine being anywhere without eventually turning to Jay and saying, "you know, we could use a change." But a couple of evenings ago I recognized that that's exactly where I was. I was living on a well-lit stage of anticipation, on the brink, like a fruit filled full with nectar nearly ready to pour out. I was living on a platform of optimism and hopefulness, where fantasy blends and becomes a plan, just before heading out on reality road. All my own projects were in that delightful early stage in which anything is possible. An editor was looking at my manuscript. Other projects - all new and exciting - were in the talking stage. I believed that some will work out and some won't. I would wait and find out which. My children, the biggest projects of all, were similarly on the brink. Both doing well, both excited about their work, both growing. Elon had started a drawing class. Erica published her first photo. Happily, both kids still live nearby so we can enjoy the glow of their pleasure. Even though they no longer say, "Look at me, Mommy, I can jump from the step!," that is what I hear. I feel proud. And grateful. And not a little amazed. The knowledge that I would agree to have this moment extend eternally, without any change, caught me quite by surprise. I don't remember ever feeling this way before. Perhaps I did, but just didn't realize how truly remarkable a feeling it is.

So this is heaven.

27 November

The icing on the Thanksgiving cake was a call from Jerusalem. S. called at 2 AM her time, while she was cooking for Shabbat. She invited us for the Seder next spring. Hearing her voice cheered me. I had been happy, surrounded by friends and family, acting all grown up in my lovely dining room...still, my dear friend S stroked me in a place only she can reach. My enjoyment of the evening became fuller after her call. My soul, like a sleeping kitten, was awakened, and stretched to receive her affection. Friendship is a powerful, gentle force.

December

4 December

Feminism

Reading *Memoirs of a Geisha*, a novel by William Golden and watching *Sex in the City*, I am struck by how little has changed in the lives of women. They are still directed by their longing for a man. The cool women in *Sex*... take a course in tantric sex (hilariously taught by the Doctors

Shapiro in their apartment). They want to know how to please a man. It's New York in the '90s, so they go to bed with their men on the first or second date, but despite their bravado, they are essentially insecure about their attractiveness, their lovability. They dread losing their youth. Above all else they are needy. Desperately needy. They are like the Geisha, painted and groomed, graceful and charming, and totally, absolutely dependent on the attention of her patron. Totally bereft without him. All of the women are nobody without a man. It almost makes one believe that the curse of Eve has stuck.

10 December

Thomas Merton is my man! In the *Seven Storey Mountain* he notes the difference between the monastic life and the rest of society:

> "Excellence, here, was in proportion to obscurity: the one who was best was the one who was least observed, least distinguished. Only faults and mistakes drew attention to the individual.
>
> The logic of the Cistercian life was, then, the complete opposite to the logic of the world, in which men put themselves forward so that the most excellent is the one who stands out, the one who is eminent above the rest, who attracts attention...
>
> The logic of worldly success rests on a fallacy: the strange error that our perfection depends on the thoughts and opinions and applause of other men!

> A weird life it is, indeed, to be living always in somebody else's imagination, as if that were the only place in which one could at last become real!"

The worldly fallacy of relying on public acclaim for personal validation runs deep and wide among us. There's no absolutely getting away from it, after all. Like babies dependent upon adult's "mirroring" for a sense of self and well-being, we need others in order to know how we're doing. It is a fallacy that we can't live without. Perhaps that is why I have always loved the legends of the "Lamedvovniks", the 36 people whose quiet goodness sustains the world. They are the pillars of the world who appear, to themselves and to the rest of us, to be just simple, ordinary folk. Real heroes go unrecognized.

22 December

Mood is such a powerful force. Even mild dysphoria infects the mind with pessimism. The error it induces is the capturing of the future: biting a problem whole makes a convincing case for starvation. Chewing and swallowing are clearly impossible. Was Kohelet (Ecclesiastes) depressed and therefore unable to see the endless flowing of the river as a source of comfort rather than despair? Part of life's beauty and nobility is that it keeps going on. I marveled at the speed with which new buds appeared in the remains of Hurricane Iniki. Trees bore both scars and new growth. Last night our community honored a family whose son had recently been brought to the hospital in handcuffs with a new diagnosis of schizophrenia. Collectively, we are Job. Like him, we persevere, and when we can't, we merely endure. Borne with grace, the struggle is noble. To triumph is to survive without bitterness.

Winter

3 January

We planned to cocoon this Shabbat, and still I was surprised at the depth of my fatigue. I dozed, read and ate the afternoon away. I was on the couch at 6:20, long after Shabbat was over, when Elon asked, "Aren't we going to say Havdalah?" Each time I awoke I was surprised still to feel tired. Each nap was very pleasing, like each slice of a fresh blueberry pie.

I read *Tuesdays with Morrie* this weekend, and made a New Year's resolution to meditate in the morning, before I get going. I can meditate on a *pasuk* (sentence) in *tehillim* (psalms), and feel that it is more immanent than conventional prayer. It is odd that spiritual practice embarrasses me. Still, "spiritual" is easier than "religious". It entails no obligations. And while obligation is, as Heschel pointed out, one of Judaism's great gifts, it bothers me to hear Orthodox Jews assert that they would never have chosen Judaism. They practice because they believe they must. That position has been elevated to indicate a high degree of faith and obedience. And, of course, it does. But it also seems to indicate a failure of growth, or a willful blindness. A child may do his homework because Dad told him to. He may do it out of love for his dad, desire for his approval, the wish to be considered a good boy and get a present, or fear of punishment for noncompliance. Any motivation will do. But by the time the child becomes an adult we hope that he would have 1) learned the content of the homework and recognized that compliance helped him to learn to read and write, and 2) incorporated the values and habits of discipline, completing tasks, and all the other process issues homework teaches. If he continues to proclaim that the value of homework is merely obedience to father, hasn't he missed the point?

4 January

It is interesting to reflect on events and people who made a difference in my life. Sometimes it appears, fallaciously, that if the relationships didn't endure or become close and ongoing, then contact didn't mean anything. Or perhaps they were just disappointing. But that is not the case. More often, a moment of contact offered a glimmer, a conversation, a touch, that moved my life on. It may become clear only years later that this person, that opportunity, was the occasion for release—or deepening—a chance to catch my breath, or focus, or shake the veils off my eyes, or let go. Resentment or regret over what was not metamorphoses into the pleasure of discovery and appreciation for what was.

5 January

Sometimes it seems that when there is a lull and one has nothing to do, problems rush in to fill the gap. Or do we just grab the problem that might otherwise get by, because it gives us something to wrestle with, and in its embrace we find meaning - or at least shelter in the distraction from - nothing. Boredom. That uncomfortable period when we are without a particular focus.

6 January

On her birthday this week she seemed warmly, delightfully happy. The pressures of school are over for the semester, the long pre-Christmas work days were over. She had a well-deserved vacation in which she made some pasta, played with her dog, Priscilla, slept late and ran errands. For her birthday she got a stuffed dog from Elon that looked exactly like Priscilla. She got professional framing for several of her photographs from us, and an onyx pendant with a diamond chip on a gold chain. She had asked for the framing - we were glad that she was proud of her work and wanted to display it. The necklace was something spontaneous and special. A gift for a young woman that was meant to say, "you are elegant and grown-up. A beautiful young woman, worthy of jewels."

Erica wears a lot of black, brown and neutrals; flattering, very art-student-y, and not unlike her mom's artless, tailored look. She spells her name, "Xeriqua," which, she explains, is more visually compelling and artistic. (The "X " is silent.) So we had "Xeriqua" spelled on her birthday cake. I hope it communicated that we are behind her as she is, who she is. I remember writing to her in my mind, and finally in her book when she was a baby. Those were long, frustrating months - a year? - between the time we learned that she was available until I finally had her in my arms. She rested there, snug and comfortable, from the first moment.

8 January

Once again my computer is malfunctioning, and I am disturbed by the inconvenience, and my own incompetence. Without printer, fax and e-mail I am out of business. I am at sea, dependent on Elon, angry at the low level of mechanical performance acceptable in the computer world. No other appliance could break down as often and still be used. Computerland is a third world country, where people shrug philosophically and keep going when the lights go out. Cyberspace is a banana republic.

Elon guides me through my computer turmoil with patience and the particular warmth that is his own. He has the gift of extraordinary empathy, since earliest childhood his ability to relate to people regardless of their ages or stations has been notable. "How come people say this is a good movie?", he asked tearfully after seeing the movie, E.T., when he was a little boy. "It's so sad." I have no doubt that he would be able to empathize with a real extraterrestrial, were he to meet one! Certainly nothing human is alien to him.

It is a wonderful gift, but not an unmixed blessing, to feel so exquisitely much.

10 January

The infant parakeet, Lacy, tries to fly with his clipped wings. He smashes blindly into the wall, and falls between the folds of pants tossed in the corner. "He's angry," interprets Elon. "He's saying, why did you let me go and hurt myself?"

11 January

The first large sheep was cloned last week. The news reported monkey clones this week. And I wonder: clones at one end...adoption at the other. Families can indeed be formed in many ways. What they share is commitment to their future. I think that may be all they share.

If you found out that you had been cloned in your sleep, would you feel an attachment to the twin who resulted? A fascination, perhaps, at how much of yourself you could see in the other. But would you feel related? Attracted? The desire to know and be known? Love? Rivalry? Although biologically twins of different ages, would she be your sister?

Perhaps one day the world will be such that all children can be reared by their biological parents. There would be no more need for adoption. Only then would there be any point in cloning.

13 January

This nondescript Sunday morning in January is the kind of day one would ordinarily forget. It is a day embedded with happiness. Like a shapely naked woman wearing an oversized gray trench coat, or a genius with awkward social skills, joy in ordinary moments is overlooked instead of given its due. The homage due is simple: recognition, gratitude, *consciousness.*

14 January

I've begun perusing *tehillim* (psalms) for sentences that speak to me as food for meditation. I'm beginning to think that the Jewish understanding of happiness is similar to the Buddhist, although it isn't given the same priority. The person of faith, it seems to be saying, lives in another reality that provides him with protection from his enemies, inner and outer. It is a way of detaching—without denying or defending crazily. Faith is enlightenment, it seems to me.

I really like Psalm 34:9 "*Ta'amu uriu ke tov Hashem...*" (Taste and see that God is good), because the word "taste" implies a direct, sensual and primitive way of contacting reality. Taste is the baby's primary encounter with the world. Taste implies pleasure and nourishment. And "taam" is used in this chapter to mean intellect or understanding. I like that the phrase that appealed to me is in a chapter that deals with David asking God to make him crazy in order to save him from the Philistine king, Avimelech. Craziness speaks volumes to me. I have seen enough of it to know that madness can indeed be a way out of an impossible situation.

The Biblical David is not the only person to have turned to madness to survive.

The second sentence I came across last night was chapter 37:3 "*B'tach b'Hashem v'asay tov. sh'chon aretz uriay emunah.*" (Trust in God and do good. Dwell in the land and be nurtured by faith.) The simplicity of the message, trust in God and do good, is a mantra. The second part of the pasuk (sentence), Dwell in the land and be nurtured by faith, is comforting. The word "*u'riay*" is from the word "shepherd" . The shepherd, that image from Psalm 23, is watching, so we can relax and feel secure. "*Riay emunah.*"

15 January

Today's meditation was "*V'ahavta et Hashem ...bichol miodecha.*" (And you shall love God, your God, with all your heart and with all your soul and with all you possess) But I couldn't stay with it because it made me anxious. It is a commandment. So I shifted to receiving love, "*Ahavat olam, beit yisrael...amcha ahavta*" (With an endless love have You loved Your people, Israel.) The receptive form felt better.

Morning meditation is filled with noise, like a room filled with a chattering crowd. Today's Shema Yisrael mantra was like an overlay, but the background noise never did turn down. It will.

16 January

Here's an idea I had for a group I'd like to try with Hillel students. The flyer might read:

Godtalk

The search for a relationship with God is the ground from which religion grows. Sometimes the noise of religious practice and politics obscures its spiritual dimension. This group will provide a nondenominational opportunity to contemplate the personal "still, small voice" within us. It will be an opportunity to share your thoughts about God and your spiritual experiences. Where relevant, we will look at our own experiences in the context of Jewish philosophical sources.

17 January

I've been tired and out of focus a lot this week. Could be PMS, the weather turning cold, not stretching after my work-outs, the gray cold of January, or just having too much discretion over my schedule. Whatever the cause, being tired for no reason arouses a latent hypochondria. I am surprised to encounter the thought, "Maybe I'm sick. Maybe there's something wrong with me that I don't know about." I banish the thought crisply, flicking at the intruder with a mental whip, moving on to my next task with serious intent. Like most women, I am dissatisfied with my body, which retains its size 14 flab despite all the exercise. But it does heal itself, which is so easy to take for granted. The neck pain I don't have this winter, as I did last. The smooth coordination of my arms and legs on the NordicTrak. Bouncing backwards and forwards on the cross-trainer, I see a drop of sweat fall from my face and it still surprises me! My body performs satisfactorily, it just doesn't look good. It's a good enough Volvo, not a sleek, late model Jaguar.

19 January

Tired again, or still tired? Being tired is a drag. I can't fathom why I feel deeply tired these mornings, today more deeply than usual. And I slip easily into sleep most nights. Why am I so tired?

20 January

Buffered by comfort food, eased into place by taxicabs and airplanes, a visit to my mother is still deeply stressful. My shoulders and neck finally relaxed when I was back home, soothed, my ordeal over. It was an ordinary visit, dominated by her depression, her dissatisfaction. She complains, demands, whines or expresses regret about every small decision. Decisions she makes and those she refuses to make are regretted equally. The wheelchair becomes heavier and harder to push when it is weighted down by her negativity.

21 January

Today I'm rested, energetic and cheerful. Could it be because yesterday Xeriqua came home from her England adventure? Insight.

22 January

Today's meditation was "*Hashem oz l'amo y'tain...bashalom.*" (God will give strength to his nation and will bless them with peace) I thought of it in terms of giving strength to fight one's internal struggle, a blessing of peace of mind, serenity. It was a pleasing choice. The surface of my mind is still wild and choppy, even when I first wake up.

The other day I realized that in all my years of parenting only two people ever gave me positive feedback. One was a stranger on an Amtrak train going from New York to Philadelphia who identified herself as a psychologist and complimented me on the way I managed 6 year old Elon and 3 year old Erica's trip together to the cafe car to buy candy. The other was A.L. who commented on how "related" I was with them (ages 7 & 10 at the time, I believe). Parenting is such important, lonely work, heavy with ambiguity and risk. I must remember to tell people what I think they're doing right.

24 January

There are days when the world, and the wonder of being in it, seem fresh. When walking down the street is a symphony of sensations, crisp breeze on my cheeks, a pastel pink quilted coat above black and white leggings on the blond woman at my left, who is concentrating on the challenge of crossing K Street. She seems oblivious to all the pleasure around us. My vision caresses the streets as I pass. The occasions of color in the store windows are sensual stops in the balance of small buildings following the taller ones at my back. I have just spent an hour baking brownies and cooking soup at home in luxurious silent solitude, savoring the time alone in part because it implies the promise of people I love around the Shabbat table at the end of a satisfying week. Each of us is growing visibly, perceptively; separate flowers joined at the root. I am headed to my office where I will listen to Christopher Parkening's guitar and Vivaldi, and know I am blessed. This is joy. And I am filled with gratitude.

28 January
Key West, Florida

Vacation reading is usually enjoyable junk. But a good writer...a good writer can make the ordinary beautiful. He can make even the ugly beautiful, which goes to show that Keats was wrong. Beauty is not truth. Not at all. John Banville's novel, *The Untouchable*, describes a degraded homosexual encounter in a dirty public lavatory, and it reads like a psalm.

Breakfast at the Cuban cafe - sweet cafe con leche and Cuban bread eaten outdoors under palms landscaped to look casual - has become our routine. In three days the waiters, she a flake, and he a Key West figure of late middle-aged fatigue, cigarette dangling from his lips, treat us like regulars. That pleases us.

Jay and I vacation with a rhythm learned over many years. We know each other and ourselves, and observe how hard it would be to vacation with other people. But here we see lots of older people traveling, some of them in groups of 4 or 6, and it looks enviable. Old friends having fun together is something I would love to see up close. Since I haven't yet seen that phenomenon in real life, it has the quality of romance. It is a flavor of life I have never tasted. I know no older people with friends, old or new. When I was a child, C.'s parents were remarkable for having friends. So it is that Jay and I vacation alone together, knowing at what point we have had enough margaritas, enough of restaurants and bad local bands, and are ready to take in a movie and eat a sandwich in our hotel room, with its unobscured ocean view and TV set. There Clinton tells us the State of the Union is strong, and so is the state of his sex life, and 77% of Americans approve. Americans are children who want Daddy to be morally perfect, of course, and are also secretly proud of his virility.

February

8 February

I'm thinking a lot about religion lately. But, then, religion has always been an important tone in my life. Even when I was most distant from it, and most rebellious against it, Judaism pervaded my life. My consciousness is Jewish, just as surely as it is female. Today religion is hot in America, and Christianity and Buddhism seem to be vying for the public soul. The struggle between their messages make for an active backdrop against which to look at my own Judaism.

9 February

A person without religious sensibility is like a colorblind person. Try explaining color to them, and you will fail. Try convincing them that color even exists, and they may think you are delusional. They argue, isn't the world enough for you as it is, in black and white and gray? Color is not "out there." It is not a quality of the object. It is a dynamic between object, subject, and the air and light between them. It is the sensation produced by light waves on the rods (or is it cones?) in the eye. You have to have the right receptors to know that color "exists."

The colorblind may live lives just as good, just as happy, just as moral, and just as wise - but lives lived in color are immeasurably richer. Even when not consciously noticed, color provides emotional tone. It brings warmth to the scene, along with depth and interest. Just think of a dramatic moment in Bergman's movie, *Fanny and Alexander*, and imagine it drained of all color. From Bergman to this morning's casual closet selection, the color palette is a constant. Like religion, it can be pale background or bold foreground.

Whether bright contrast or subtle hues, color is seasoning that stimulates and satisfies. We see it all day, and it drenches our dreams at night.

The colorblind experience everything in life but this. Deprived of color daily, deprived of it in their imaginations and even in their dreams, the colorblind may believe that color doesn't exist at all.

10 February

If the ultimate judge of the philosophy and values of a community is the society it creates, Orthodox Judaism has something to worry about. On a grand scale, it is the Orthodox God-fearing institutions that produced ideological murderers in our time: Baruch Goldstein and Yigal Amir. On a local scale here in Washington a day school principal has breached his contract for a better deal elsewhere, leaving a small school vulnerable and unstable. "The contract is unenforceable," he announced. A lawyer friend who called on his behalf noted, "that's how it's done in this industry."

We seem to raise our children, especially our boys, and most especially, I would argue, the boys who remain in the ethnic, family-style, sheltered educational environment, to be narcissistic. They are so special, our beloved, spoiled children. They get the message that because of their specialness, because they are so smart, so charming, so well-intentioned and good, that ordinary rules don't apply to them. Mom and Dad may say no at first, but who can resist their pleas? In these cases, it seems that the idea that someone may say 'no' to them never entered their mind. The principal was surprised - shocked! - by the school board's resistance. It never occurred to him that he was responsible to his contract. After all, he had done a good job, hadn't he? Who would begrudge him the next step in his career? That the school might have its own priorities was something he had not considered.

Maybe narcissism is an occupational hazard of religion. What about the Catholic Church insisting on crosses at Auschwitz? Or having a tantrum - closing its holy sites - when it was forced to share the plaza in Nazareth with a Mosque? Like the principal denying responsibility for breaching his contract, the Vatican refused to take responsibility for its tantrum. Instead it blamed Israel for creating conflict! (Israel crafted the compromise in which both Moslems & Christians ended up with some, but not all, of what they wanted.)

Back in Silver Spring, the firestorm that raged because leadership insisted that a contract be honored revealed the community to be a dysfunctional family. "He's unhappy," people said. "It isn't good to keep someone in a position they don't want." I translated that as, "The kid will sulk if he doesn't get his way. Don't upset him. Let's dance around to make it work out the way he wants." It's a dynamic I know too well. The stress of maintaining an unpopular decision perceived to be "hard" against a popular man disturbed Jay's sleep. It infiltrated my dreams in the form of a young, black hatted man, part of a delegation visiting my house, who rummaged through my pantry when I left the room. The narcissism of that invasion, the entitlement that recognized only his agenda and disregarded my boundaries, infuriated me. My tirade against him in my dream woke me up. This degree of narcissism is blinding. On a communal scale it is self-destructive. Surely Judaism is not an "industry" that can function when an agreement—a contract—words—are not honored.

Then there was the Woodside bat mitzvah (or bas mitzvah, as the speakers pronounced it, despite the years they spent living and attending school in Israel). It was a warm, enjoyable, well-planned event, redolent of good feeling and authenticity. I knew many people. Since I was close to the family, I was also the "official" photographer. Then why was it so clear to me that I did not belong? I thought of my kids' experiences of not fitting in, and understood them. I look different, towering over the 200 or so Jewish women in the room, as physically unique (in my mind, at least) as the one Black guest (when she watched the clumsy folk dancers next to her, did she think, "God, these women can't move!"). Speech patterns pockmarked by "*im yirtzeh hashem*" (God willing) and "*baruch hashem*" (thank God) made me think of the SNL satire of the evangelical woman who calls on Jesus so often and for such minutia that he finally visits her in person to tell her to leave him alone! I recognized a subgroup which I visit, but to which I do not belong. I felt sorry to see the older sister, only 21 and in school, bearing a snood to cover her hair and a pregnant belly. Life will be so much harder for her now. These are all women who work hard, whose standards for a good, full and rich life involve constant effort and service. But it is a life self-selected by people who made choices, and it is a life lived more consciously than most, blessed by literacy, prosperity and strong family and communal ties.

12 February

Religion aims to rescue humanity. Christianity promises salvation from death and its terrors. Its end is salvation. Buddhism offers salvation from suffering and confusion. Its end is enlightenment and serenity. Judaism begins with salvation. The birth of the nation of Jews was salvation. As slaves, we knew fear, suffering, the threat of extinction from which we were saved. Saved by "grace," we were graciously given a means of enlightenment as well, plus 40 years of solitude in which to meditate and consolidate the gifts. A nation of survivors from the start, we began with the prize, and the challenge of what follows.

Survivors are convinced they were saved for a reason. They are energized by the challenge of having to make their lives mean something. They are more awake, less prone to taking life for granted, than those who have not escaped or overcome significant threat. They often feel the need to give something back, build a monument, make a difference. "Survivors' guilt" is as likely to be survivors' appreciation, survivors' memory, survivors' enlightenment, salvation.

13 February
Chapel Hill, NC

A.L. walks daily with two women friends. They move briskly along their landscaped, upscale neighborhoods, admiring gardens and architecture. One day they met two elderly men who lived on one block. The first was pleased by the way the women admired his rosebushes. One day he gallantly cut a rose for each of them to take home. The old man and the walkers became friends in a neighborly, front yard kind of way. He looked forward to the days their walking route passed his way. They smiled in anticipation of meeting him.

The second man's garden had beautiful shrubs that the walkers admired as they struck up a conversation. He regaled them grayly with the difficulty of gardening in that spot. Delivery trucks got stuck backing into the driveway, he complained; some of the cuttings died. He'd just as soon live in a condo and not be bothered with it all. Exasperation and disappointment surrounded him like fog.

Two men gardened on the same fertile street, but clouds cast shadows over one, while the other was blessed with rain.

15 February

The Eighth Intelligence

Howard Gardner posits the existence of 7 dimensions of intelligence, far more than the two or three we used to think there were. He calls them linguistic, logical-mathematical, spatial, musical, bodily-kinesthetic, interpersonal and intrapersonal. I'd add an eighth, religious intelligence. An individual can be creative and expressive in song and dance, basketball and prose, music and sculpture. She may demonstrate interest in and inclination toward math, appreciation for the "elegance" of a theory and gracefulness in acting or teaching. Religious intelligence differs from interpersonal intelligence in its choice of audience. Where the writer and painter, dancer and teacher "perform" for an audience of peers and the public, the religious thinker "performs" for peers and for the Other. All are expressive, they dance and write because it pleases them to do so, because they have something to say, because they are moved to take action, because they are making something. Each of the intelligences is a language in which a person can say "I am." The religious intelligence deals with moral issues (as the sculptor and dancer deal with space), with issues of transcendence, with ultimate issues.

Verbal ability enters into it (a philosopher and a poet may or may not have religious intelligence) and so does a talent for serenity. When Jim Fowler talks about "faith development" he comes close to the same conclusion.
Almost all people walk, but we vary greatly in our bodily-kinesthetic intelligence. Everyone thinks about and relates

to God and the questions of right-wrong, good-evil, pain and suffering, meaning and death. But we vary greatly in our religious intelligence.

16 February

Today I'm procrastinating about preparing for the psychology of religion class. It starts in 3 weeks, and I'll be away for the last week. The books I borrowed from the library last month to prepare for the class are overdue. Because I didn't renew them in time they have to be carried back, a fine paid, and then renewed. What is this procrastination about? I'll take a break, go out for a coffee, and think about it.

17 February

What about death? Death didn't come into the world because of the sin of Adam. It was already there, he just didn't know it. Otherwise, why would Eden have contained the tree of life? Animals die, have labor pains and suffer loss, just like we do. They work to feed themselves and protect their young, just like we do. Like us they suffer, but they don't contemplate suffering. Consciousness of impermanence was the curse.

Adam and Eve were like two or three year old children who know the names of things. They are driven by curiosity and attachment, as well as pain and pleasure, but they are not conscious. They are not aware of sex, death and the anxieties they arouse in work, love and childrearing. Before "knowledge" one works for the pleasure of mastery, or to be part of the group, or for approval, but without the anxious awareness that one's life depends upon it. Before "knowledge" there are attachment and love which feel good, and there are separation and loneliness which feel bad. But there is no self-reflection. The curses grow from the awareness of death. Death, for the Bible, is evil. The knowledge of good and evil —therefore choose life.

18 February

Even a cold can get you down. A chest cough with the mildest of sore throat and sore ears just makes me want to rest. It always seems remarkable to find myself without energy, unable to focus...just plain sick. It is the narcissism of the well, an alienation from the reality of our own frailty. Even now, I feel that taking it easy is self-indulgent. It is okay to do that, since no one suffers any real loss, but I believe that if I needed to I could gather myself and act and work as if I were completely well. Since I don't have to "give into it," I am not "really" sick. Not really vulnerable. Not really mortal. My narcissism is intact; I'm not "really" sick.

19 February

Sometimes I think that Christianity and Islam are the public relations or marketing departments of Judaism's product, monotheism. By placing a human being close to the center (Deified in Christianity and not in Islam - nevertheless, both pronounce the name of a man when they state the central tenet of their faith), they make God more user-friendly. When the Rabbis obsess about apparently insignificant details of observance they are as editors who dot i's and cross t's, fuss over punctuation and whether the spacing is correct in the bibliography. The editors know that content - the story - is what the book is about. But they also know that the book's enduring value depends upon attention to detail. Nitpicking serves the product.

23 February

I'm back from Wyoming, where a Jew invented the ten gallon hat.

I'm so lucky to have a great deal of travel planned for this season. I feel blessed...and daunted, as well, with the recognition of how much grunt work is involved in the good things in life.

The conference in Laramie, Wyoming turned out to be a warmly memorable experience. The relatively small group of presenters, who also shared some travel problems (we tried to call them "adventures"), got to know one another. There was the pleasant couple from London, and the soft Mississippian, the boy-from-Brooklyn, the Public Health Service shrink, and the sad sack from Duluth. G.D., the gentle organizer who wore western string ties and reminded me of a cartoon character from the Simpsons, turned out to be a lone operator (euphemistically referred to as being in private practice) who lives in a trailer park. His success in arranging an international conference —in Laramie, in February, no less —seemed all the more remarkable for knowing that. When else would I have had a chance to meet J.C. from Jackson Hole, Wyoming, who along with consulting to the local hospital on trauma cases goes out to the mountains with the team of climbing search and rescuers. As I am planning for my trip to Israel, she takes off for New Zealand where her husband will participate in the Iron Man triathalon. Then, after rendezvousing with her college student daughter in Fiji for a few days, she will head out to Colorado to train with her show horse (dressage). At 51, she's got the slender body of an athlete, and the lined face of a nature lover. She was moved by my first presentation, "The Poetry of Recovery", which got a surprisingly warm reception. To J.C., I seem unusual! I guess I am, too.

24 February
an e-mail to my friend

Dear A.L.,

Well, I'm back from the big sky country of Wyoming, which I enjoyed more than I expected. The conference was very enjoyable; with about 80 attendees there was enough content to be interesting, and enough interaction to really get to know different people. One of the things I like about disaster mental health is that the field has almost no career opportunities, so everyone in it is there because they're really interested. Kind of like a hobby. And I always get to know people whose experiences couldn't be more different from my own: a psychologist-climber who does search and rescue in avalanches, for example.

Since returning I've begun tying up all the details for our Israel trip. We leave March 7, and plan to return during Passover. I've been waiting for a moment to tell you my impressions of one of the books you sent me, *Meeting Jesus Again for the First Time.*

The book touched me in a funny way. You remember that Borg makes a big point about Jesus emphasizing God as compassionate, as if that were a radical departure from the Judaism in which he was raised. Well, my Hebrew name is Ruchama (compassionate one), the same word he keeps returning to, the same root as the word for womb. So I took it personally, and I was surprised at the notion that the centrality of God as compassionate could be anything but the most traditionally Jewish. The directive to imitate God by imitating his compassionate qualities is the classical interpretation in the Judaism I know. It is a refrain of the Yom Kippur liturgy.

Some things just seemed off-base. Borg makes a big case for the idea that Jesus was marginal because he socialized with marginal people, especially shepherds. Now, I don't know anything about the sociology of Israel in Jesus' time, but shepherds have a very positive image in the Bible. Moses was a shepherd when God first spoke to him from the burning bush. David was a shepherd when he was chosen for leadership. The Lord is a shepherd for the Psalmist. I would argue that the Jewish image of a shepherd is practically one of preparation for religious leadership, combining as it does solitude, openness to nature, and compassion and responsibility for others.

Borg's rejection of what he calls the purity laws seems to

rely on his interpretation of those rituals as exclusionary. "Purity" is term used often in the context of sexual behavior ("family purity" is the category of laws that direct married couples to create space between them for part of each month, making the return to intimacy fresh). My understanding is that he is correct in the idea that holiness in Judaism always involves making distinctions or separating, i.e, separating the holy from the profane. It seems to me that just as the fully actualized individual needs both connection and individuation, so does the complete religious system provide for connection - and what is compassion but the ability to connect to another? - and individuation. Holiness is a kind of individuation, a separation. The message is that an aspect of holiness is achieved by creating a separation from (non-attachment?)- by not being enslaved by- one's passions.

Man's yearning for union with God is met with a method for imitating His ways - both by compassion, and by separation. Both means mimic His ways, for He is compassionate and close to his creatures, but separate from them. Like a marriage in which the couple can be intimate but must also be individuals, a covenantal system, in which Man is a partner with God, requires the capacity for separation as well as connection.

The overriding meaning of the purity rituals, I believe, is life affirmation. Judaism developed in a pagan world and emphatically rejected its celebration of death. Not only did the Jewish priests, in contrast to the pagan ones, not preside over death rituals, they were not even permitted to have contact with the dead. Purity rituals symbolize a distancing from death, and a method of life-affirmation.

Some, but not all, of the rituals, involved sacrifices in the

Temple. And that, of course, is where corruption became an issue. Certainly the corruption of the priesthood was a fatal flaw. Jesus' criticism, like those of the prophets, pointed out how dangerous the combination of money, power and religion can be. The hypocrisy of ostentatiously religious people continues to be a problem.

Whew - this turned out to be a sermon! Well, the book made an impression on me!

What did we do before e-mail?

Love,
Renee

25 February

Hitaneg al Hashem, v'yitayn l'cha mishalot leebechah. (Rejoice in God and he will fulfill your heart's desires)

If you are at a place where you delight in (enjoy) God, then all the wishes of your heart will be fulfilled. My take on that is that you will be transformed, your desires will be transformed, you will be the sort of person who is high on God, focused on the High and eternal, so your heart will - by definition - be satisfied. What an idea.

26 February

Haziman Katzar Haavodah Mirubah, uBaal Habayit Dochef.

(There is little time, there is a great deal of work to be done, and the Master of the House urges us on)

How do you know how much is enough? The Jew's overachievement has been ascribed to Galut, to the neurotic feeling of being "chased by the man with a gun," but it is deeper than that. It is the half-angel part calling to the half-animal part saying," you can be better." "Pay attention." "Try harder." It is Ecclesiastes' resistant, "why bother, all is vanity," confronting the work still to be done. The anxiety over wasting time, one's only real resource, and the paradox of consciousness. Time is wasted if one is unconscious, just busy, just doing. But consciousness, just being or being reflective and mindful, takes time and appears unproductive. The illusion of appearances...or the illusion of productivity? Travel too far down that road (or take the wrong turn) and you come to despair. It is a quandry.

What is "avodah" (work) in this sentence? An ambiguous word, traditionally translated in the text as prayer (religious work, sacrifices). Are we being urged to hurry and take time from our short, distraction-and task-filled life to work on this other work, where there is so much to do? The Master of the "house" pushes us forward in this work. (Time, after all, is the real house we live in during our stay on this earth.) What does this work consist of? Things that can only be done while there is time, and in which the Master is invested.

"Work" is wonderful in its ambiguity. It could mean that if you do your tasks mindfully, with the recognition of the Master's urging, it becomes Avodah, a work of holiness.

March

1 March

What if we reversed the figure and ground, and saw our experiences as having independent existences, instead of our selves? Then dreams would be travelers, and our sleeping minds merely the medium for a moment's stop. Moods, emotions, ideas, and feelings would be the figures, traveling as naturally as do currents through the water, winds through the air, or seasons over the globe. We would be to them as the water, churned by forces it neither "owned" nor created, or the land where a tornado just happened to touch down.

2 March

Although I wish my friends and acquaintances good health, I am touched to be the one they call to help them out when they're not well. I babysat for one friend's child when she went to the ER with chest pains (happily, no heart problem was found, and the cause of the pains is still unknown). The next day I picked up another child from kindergarten when both her parents were laid up with the flu. I felt warmed by the connections that brought me an opportunity to help in those ways. It was another example of Jay's grandfather's wisdom: "whatever you do, you do for yourself."

3 March

I woke up last Sunday on my back with my arms stretched out above my head. The sun streamed in through the half-open blinds and I felt I understood how the puppy, Priscilla, feels when she rests in that same position. The satisfaction of a relaxation that lets you leave your body wide open, because you need no protection. All that day I remained a puppy in a happy household. It's a pleasing image: a mood in which all is agreeable, nothing is missing or needed. Waking up rested, warm and outstretched is a moment to return to. A meditation.

4 March

A cold or flu has me in its grip, despite my best efforts with a cortisone inhaler and codeine cough medicine. I wake up aching and tired, and I see my personality deteriorate into irritability. Even this low level of discomfort, lasting just about a week, has a deforming effect. Unless I'm perfectly healthy to the end, I'm afraid I will be a crabby old woman!

Yesterday I was walking home clutching my coat against the wind, deeply immersed in fantasy. An Indian man walked toward me and observed with a smile, "you look happy." I had been thinking thoughts of disengagement. The Buddhists had a point; warm detachment is a platform for happiness.

6 March

But it's impossible to maintain. A butterfly's wing caressed my skin, a pebble fell in the forest, an e-mail note appeared, my child's face was pale, my friend unresponsive - and my heart reattached at the aorta, pounding its existence with the passion and intensity of a hurricane. Then Detachment became an illusion. My blood and its pulse declared themselves reality.

Jay and I each had a project for our month in Israel. Jay's was to photograph the Old City of Jerusalem and parts of Jordan. I was going to "learn". My challenge was to examine conflict resolution in Jewish history. I wanted to learn the lessons of the past , to promote Jewish unity in the future.

10 March
JERUSALEM

A tear slid down my face during my conversation with Steven Wald this morning. The founder of the Conservative Yeshiva across the street, who grew up in a Reform family, gave up his dream of becoming a Dayan (religious court judge) because he lacks "yichus"(inherited family status). The Yeshiva world would never accept him, he recognized, no matter how learned, how good, how pure he might become. A tear slid down my face, a tear of shame, because he was right.

I guess there'll be no more Rabbi Akivas.

13 March

There must be something in the cool dry air on these hills, this sacred space of Jerusalem. Shortly after D.'s Bar Mitzvah, his late father appeared to S. in a dream to tell her that D.'s tephilin needed checking, and they turned out, indeed, to be pasul (to have imperfections that invalidated their use). She sees the hand of God in every coincidence, and every lucky break.

Today a short, dumpy woman with a southern accent chatted with me in the lobby of the Kings Hotel. Since God called her to be a missionary, she happily explained, she's been to Fiji, to Russia, and elsewhere. A few years ago He told her she'd get to Israel, and here she is. No organization funds her; she just does His work and He provides.

Both women sound a lot alike to me. Certain they both feel surrounded by and guided by a personal benevolent force in another dimension. Both are moved to share their understanding for the greater good of all. And they both seem very happy. *V'hitaneg al Hashem, v'yimaleh mishalot libecha (*Rejoice in God, and He will fulfill your heart's desire*)*. They would both probably be deeply offended by the very idea of any similarity between them.

14 March

Jerusalem is a theme park. Ben Yehudah Street and King George are summer camp for teenagers and young adults; where their parents can send them to a safe, Jewish environment in which to experience budding independence. Rechavia, a Jerusalem neighborhood, is Florida for New York, Orthodox retirees, where shiurim (lectures) predominate, instead of early-bird specials, and take-out food is plentiful.

My experience of Jerusalem reminds me of New York; I enjoy them both for their ethnicity, familiarity, nostalgia and stimulation. Filled with smart people, ideas, creativity, and ideals...both are good places to visit. The Old City is like Williamsburg, Virgina, an historical setting populated by people in costumes of another age, plying trades of a different time. The dignified black-clad man with a long white beard who stopped to offer us help with directions sounded like he might have been from somewhere near Ohio. The incongruity of his voice and casual, very American, manner with his appearance made us smile. The incongruity felt artificial - like when an actor steps out of character and reminds you that it is, after all, only a play.

Again, as in Eilat back in '91, Israel feels very small and cramped. I am surprised now, as I was then, to see how the lack of space, the enclosedness of Israel imposes on my consciousness. In Wyoming the wide open spaces had a soothing effect, as if one's soul could expand in the space. The way stretching refreshes the body, that's how open space relaxes the soul. The narrow streets of the Jewish Quarter have charm, but no air to breathe. Just as walls and corners curtail and shape one's movement in space, so do the pervasive social barriers restrict every movement. A visitor once asked E., who lives in the Old City, whether her children played with their Arab neighbors. "Do they play with Arab children?!— They don't even play with the children who go to the other Dati (Religious) school!!!", was her astonished reply.

15 March

All of Israel, in fact, all of Jewry, should be like the scene in the library yesterday. We went to the Judaica Reading Room at the Hebrew University library in Givat Ram, and spent the day researching my project. There we wandered among a group comprised of every style of Jew: Israeli and immigrant; a Chasid with rolled peyot; kipot of various sizes, colors and materials; bareheaded men and secular women; religious couples; and women with their hair covered in a variety of ways. Everyone studied, searched, and read, helped by the bewigged librarians with their heavy American accents, clerked by the older Israeli with a crocheted *kipah*. He politely asked that, if we were able to, would we be so good as to return our books to their places when we were done? The staff was uniformly gentle and helpful - in the Xerox room, the coat room. Everyone smiled a gentle smile. "Did you find the restaurant?" , the *shomer* (guard) at the door inquired when we returned. There was no trace of Israeli irritability, impatience, or bureaucratic hassling. "You aren't a student?," the Xerox-room cashier asked, although my ignorance, confusion and clumsiness surely made that clear. She wanted to give me every chance to take advantage of a possible discount. It was a most satisfying day. This is what it might mean to feel at home among Jews, in

Zion. Where everyone is accepted and cared for, no one is criticized, the rules are reasonable, not demanding or arbitrary. Where people feel free and warmly supported to explore and relate to Yahadut (Judaism) in their own way. Yesterday at Givat Ram I saw that it was possible.

16 March

Aunt S, sick with the flu and looking quite a bit older, was moved by my resemblance to my father (which apparently increases as I age) to talk about her relations with our family, back when she lived in Washington Heights. She arrived in the U.S. alone for the first time to marry a man 24 years her senior and join a family she had never met.

She recalled my father as the only one in the family who could get it together to meet the ship and welcome her. She remembered him as having been kind to her. I recall him as a frustrated and unhappy man. She never saw him angry, but acknowledged how frustrated he had been, stuck in an occupation he hated, and not earning enough to make ends meet. Later, she agreed that he had been unhappily married. Was he kind? I remember gentle moments, funny moments, and emotional moments. But I would never have described him as particularly kind. It's nice to know someone remembers him that way.

17 March

Israel vs. Aryeh Deri is the O.J. Simpson trial of this country. With potential for riots, like those that followed the Simi Valley-Rodney King verdict. The judgment rang with Torah words: *shochad* (bribery), *mirmah* (fraud), *aveirah* (felony). Pronounced guilty, Deri blessed God "*al harah kimoh al hatovah*." (for bad things that happen, as well as for the good) Then all the other politicians expressed their sympathy with his pain and that of his wife and children. And all proclaimed loyalty to the rule of law. Amen Selah.

18 March

Watching TV is less of a waste of time when it includes working on my Hebrew. When I sit in the library I have the feeling that working on my project is more like swimming than like building. I swim through ideas - a chapter on ethical wills, a chapter in a book on ancient religious symbols - and lazily swim back to the topic. The distractions are no less interesting than the original topic. Having a topic, in fact, enables me to pursue the distractions. One can't just swim; one must choose a direction.

My sweet tooth expands when I'm anxious, I notice, and as it does when I'm lonely. Israel feeds my sweet tooth, encouraging its expansion. Tonight Jay is in Jordan, both kids are in the States, and I'm here in Jerusalem snacking on honey-soaked pastries, and little Japanese kumquats, which can be eaten entirely, including the peel. Yesterday's bittersweet chocolate bar is the chaser, washed down by Wissotzky's fruity tea.

21 March

Our weekend in Tzfat began with a walk down ancient, narrow, steep streets looking for the shul we had been told had wonderful singing on Friday night. We asked a man for directions. "Are you here for Shabbat?" he asked. When we said yes he thrust a warm package toward us. "Here. Have this cake. Enjoy your stay—Shabbat Shalom!" And off he went, having set the tone for the Garfinkels and Landaus 30th anniversary celebration at the Rimon Inn.

22 March

And the end of my productive couple of hours in the Shoken library today I chatted with the librarian. He, a freelance researcher and I were the only three in the library. We talked about my project, about conflict and division in Jewish history. A religious man, he discussed the "compromises" necessary to befriend - and break bread with - secular people. We talked about Christianity, about missionaries, about Aryeh Deri's supporters' unwitting message in calling him a Passover sacrifice...then the librarian let down his guard. "Who says we're so right?", he asked. "Judaism is hard to leave, so I am not leaving. I keep what I keep. I like to learn about it, it is good to study...but as a religion?'—he shrugged.

The scene makes a funny story. It's a recognizable scenario in the Litvish tradition. But in the actual moment I could feel the man's genuine pain. I resonated to the conflict felt by a mind that can't break through, and resists breaking out.

24 March

Sign on the monkey cage at Km 101on the Arava Road: "*Kaan lo intifada...*" - There's no intifada here. Don't throw stones at the monkey.

27 March

Last night I had my own private Haredi (Ultra-Orthodox) session. After a couple of hours of conversation I understand just how far apart the Haredi and secular really are. The Haredi need to proselytize comes not only from personal conviction, but from the best of intentions - to help another Jew find a good life in this world, and in the next. I could reinterpret some of what was said to suit my own spiritual leanings, I could empathize with much of the rest. But I reached my limit at the story of the $7,000 fertility blessing from the Mikubal (Mystic). I laughed and shook my head. "I'm too much the Mitnaged's (Rationalists, who opposed the rise of the Hasidic movement) daughter to go for the blessing stuff." It was clear that the charlatan was charging for his work, in the grand tradition of religious exploitation (and one that gave rise to Protestantism). Believers have a perfect system; they explain the donation as a necessary step in preparing the supplicant to receive the blessing. The Mikubal's special sight saw that. He didn't withhold the blessing out of self interest, God forbid - he merely didn't want to waste a blessing that wouldn't work because of the supplicant's penury! For the believer there are no conditions that warrant unbelief.

This morning Jay, sensing my restlessness while we ran errands together, urged me to go on to the library. He said, "You're a scholar, you have things to do. I'll take care of it." In the Jeshurun library my spirits lifted. I am alienated from Israel except when I'm learning, or interacting with others in the library, or connecting with my friends. I was happy to read that J.B. Soloveitchik validated my feelings of connecting through study. He saw the yearning of the intellect for knowledge and understanding as a thirst, as natural a medium for connecting with the Divine as emotional ecstasy. Let's hear it for the Mitnagdim, whose minds yearn, even as their hearts struggle with despair. And for David the librarian - who had never seen me before but let me borrow the book, as long as I said I'd bring it back tomorrow. I did bring it back, of course, and we chatted amiably. It turned out that he went to Yeshiva Rambam, just two years behind me.

When I roam the libraries I connect interpersonally, perhaps not with God, but with the community of writers and thinkers who have filled the library with their ideas. I touch them and feel connected, as if in conversation. But I don't have an organic connection to the country of Israel. I recognize, sadly, that I am a Galut Jew, never truly at home anywhere. I wish it were otherwise, but it is not. I am most at home in the kingdom of ideas.

31 March

While relating his story of having been bumped and rerouted by Air Canada, Elon said, "The man told me I couldn't get to Israel. I said, 'Only God can keep me from Israel!'" He meant it.

Spring

2 April

Spring cleaning is an emotional concept. It is the relief of removing relationships that don't work and ideas of need that are enslaving. Spring cleaning reveals the essential that has been covered with dust, mold, and the customary. The light-of the longer day, the warmer season- is the warm glow that had been hidden and is now revealed. It appears rested, younger. Some anxiety remains after the cleaning, for who knows what will happen tomorrow, or this afternoon for that matter? But the essential is secure, and most things can neither be predicted nor controlled, merely dealt with as they come.

I will listen to more music, ride my bike, and clean out my rolodex.

Spring fever's less lovely symptom is the urge to clean house. One wishes to sweep out all the mess, and leave the pristine remainder lying gamely in neat compartments, ready, but not anxious, to be used. Spring fever is being obsessed with ideas, tangled like pantyhose thrown carelessly in the drawer, that cry out for sorting and discarding, sorting and discarding, until the final few worth keeping are quietly folded.

Then the drawer can be slid shut, with satisfaction and relief.

3 April

Walking along the Tel Aviv beach today, rolling the balls of my feet in the fine sand, I repeated my favorite mantra *pasuk* (sentence): *v'hitaneg al hashem, v'yitayn licha mishalot libaychem (*Delight in God, and He will fulfill your heart's desires.*)*. It occurred to me that I can love God, even though I don't approve of everything He does.

4 April

Nature knows compassion. It knows compassion and attachment, nurturing and generosity. It knows altruism...and love. But it is cruel because it is ignorant of justice. That was Judaism's fierce objection to paganism. Neither nature worship, nor rejection of nature, but the marriage of nature with justice is worthy of man.

Schulweis suggests that *Elohim* is the God of nature, who set the universe in motion and is impersonal. *Adonai* is the personal aspect of God, who relates to prayer and individuals. It is pleasing to think of both as integral aspects of a unity. But we are still left with a God who hears cries of pain and is moved, but does not (or cannot, being prevented by His laws of nature and commitment to free will) act.

5 April

During my first years of elementary school I preferred, and was a better student of, Jewish studies compared to the secular. Mom suggested that it was caused by the schedule; the morning was devoted to Judaica when, she opined, children were alert and rested. By afternoon, when math, science, English and social studies were taught, young children are becoming tired and restless. The school day dragged on until 4:30. Even at the time I wasn't sure I agreed with the explanation. *Chumash* and *Rashi* were just deeper than arithmetic. They invited questioning and challenge that American Literature couldn't possibly entertain. You could fantasize and swim in the stories, argue with the rules, play with the words, engage the heroes, and even God himself. In "English," by contrast, we little Brooklyn kids learned that New York State was known for dairy farms. And they expected us to believe that stuff!!!

6 April

If one could maintain an attitude of expectant curiosity, of optimistic openness, under more circumstances, happiness would be increased. Then life would be an adventure, and we would be as travelers who wake up in the morning rested and quite happy to see what that day's experience will be. Not like the tourist who has a checklist of sites and will be disappointed if the Louvre is closed on Tuesday, but the traveler who explores. Everything is new to that traveler. All is noticed, recognized, studied, and appreciated. For the good traveler judgment is superfluous. A bad experience illuminates and instructs, even if one wishes not to repeat it.

But some things just matter too much. With them, I am not a traveler, but a farmer whose sweat, ingenuity and heartbeat sow the field, blessing it with loving attention. The farmer anxiously examines the buds, prays for rain and sun and the miracle of the next harvest.

7 April

A few micrograms of sodium escaped from my body under the intense Mediterranean sun, and left a pain behind my eyes. The nausea and diarrhea were debilitating enough to make me consider delaying my flight home. But a salty Greek salad helped some, and a large bag of potato chips completed the job. Just a tiny bit of salt can made the difference between wretched and well.

10 April

While riding her bike to school this morning, Xeriqua was hit by a car making an illegal left turn. Happily, the physics were in her favor, and all her lovely parts are intact. If the facts had been just slightly different - a little more speed, a little less angle - it might have been tragic. Thank God it was the way it was.
A little more speed, a little less angle. A little less salt, a

trace of *chametz*. Life is lived on the edge - *gesher tzar me'od.* (Life is a narrow bridge).

13 April

It's a gray Sunday morning, still clean of *chametz*, although we "switched back" last night. I was a little sorry to wrap up those once-a-year utensils that remain new for *Pesach* no matter how many years old they are. Spring and *Nissan*, the "first" month, do feel like a beginning, although I can't explain why. The obvious agricultural explanation shouldn't be relevant to my urban experience, but new year is how I feel. It is the refreshment of *Pesach*.

"G Strings," an all guitar program on WPFW is perfect for the moment. It is the polar opposite of the usual Washingtonian-at-home-on-Sunday-morning media activity, watching the noisy TV news analysts shout at each other and pontificate. I treasure the quiet. Although we had lovely guests for lunch yesterday, I spent many quiet hours this weekend reading Isaac Bashevis Singer's, *Shadows on the Hudson.* The writing was a Yiddish stew so rich in multicolored flavors that I wanted simultaneously to linger over each mouthful and rush on to taste the next. In this novel, Singer moved on from his usual concerns with imps and demons and the follies of broken refugees to address directly all the big questions: Is God both all-powerful and good? How should one live? Love, passion, the co-existence of the noble and holy with the petty and foolish —all in the same individual....Singer showed us what he saw and what he thought about it. His character, Grien, finally comes to a resolution that, like the end of *Kohelet* (Ecclesiastes), satisfies our need for closure, but almost seems an addendum. The story is about thrashing about, the struggle to be. The wish to be whole, happy, and worthy of respect. None of the characters is evil. All of them suffer and most inflict pain, pain they deeply regret, as they pursue happiness, or merely survival.

14 April

Mrs. B., my former patient whom I had given up for dead last fall, called me today. She needs to move to a health care center, and wants to give me her "good" china. She plaintively admitted that there are some things so hard to give up, like her 30-year-old wide-brimmed black straw Panama hat. It's good as new, she said, and still in its original box. When she wore it last, to a garden party, she got lots of compliments. Some things are so hard to give up.

"Why not hang it on the wall of your room, so you can look at it?", I suggested.

"Oh, no! I couldn't bear to see it get dusty and faded."

Some things are impossible to give up.

16 April

The morning news informed me of the huge expected increase in single older women by the year 2025. In both developing and developed countries, women outlive men. Many of those older women will be poor. I visualized a scene of streets filled with thin, bent, white-haired women, walking slowly, carrying small shopping bags. Their clothing fitted poorly. Numbers are not all that count, and while many of those women will be poor, many will have economic clout, too. What will a female dominated society be like?

18 April

I lay naked this morning, wrapped in a towel on the tiled middle tier of the steam bath, watching the room fill with steam. As the steam filled the room, what had been clear began to blur, then fade. I watched as the steam, which is nothing at all, obfuscated the reality that was right in front of my eyes. I lay there alone, relaxed, thinking of all the steam I generate that fills me with swirling vapor of no substance, rendering me blind to the reality in which I exist. I thought, I am like steam myself, my life evanescent, fleeting, and insubstantial. But soothing. Warming. Comforting for a moment...then gone.

20 April

I was so pleased this morning when L. told me my presence had "filled her up" yesterday when she was feeling down. I am pleased to be able to connect at times in a way that gives strength, comfort, encouragement, or nourishment to the other person. I did not feel particularly giving or encouraging during that conversation, but I was present. (Steam may only be steam, but when it is there it is not absent.)

I am going to empty my files before my birthday. Get rid of as much as I can, and organize the rest more simply. Thinking about that makes me feel lighter and more integrated.

21 April

I felt entirely comfortable with our having invited ourselves to our friends' seder this year. Giving and taking are both required to keep the pot cooking. I don't experience the false pride of the needy, who are afraid to ask, nor the hesitance of the shy, who wonder if anyone really wants their company. Just as I mean it when I tell others, "of course you can bring a guest," I assume others are genuinely gracious. Fortune is a wheel, "*galgal chozer ba'olam* (a wheel that continues to turn in the world).

On my way to work today I was thinking about bringing our leftover matzah to a soup kitchen, and was mulling generally about how to act with more compassion in everyday life, when I passed a homeless man on the sunny street. So I took him to lunch.

He was in the prime panhandling location on the M street bridge between Foggy Bottom and Georgetown, where I often pass beggars and experience a moment of unease. Earl held a sign that announced, "homeless and hungry." I impulsively said, "If you're hungry, come with me and I'll buy you something to eat." With some ambivalence (he'd have preferred the cash), he stashed his basket behind a bush, picked up his backpack, and walked me to Furin's Cafe, careful to walk on the outside in a gentlemanly fashion. He selected chicken shish-kabob and salad to go, because he was worried about the safety of his basket, and a bottle of mystic fruit punch. On the way out he meekly asked for some cash as well, and I declined.

It was an unsatisfying experience all around. But at least he had a good lunch.

22 April

The rampage of two high school students in Littleton, Colorado has the whole country depressed. Concern for Albanian refugees faded in the glare of healthy, beautiful white middle class students in the affluent outdoorsy suburb of Denver, surrounded by the Rocky Mountains, lying dead and riddled with holes on the evening news. It seemed to have been an elaborate suicide plan, made by a couple of miserable geeky outsiders. Before doing themselves in they would show their tormenters, those whom they envied or merely hated, just how effective their rage could be. To be or not to be was the only question, and it questions our entire culture. It was a terrorist attack with no point, on the anniversary of the Oklahoma City bombing. The day was said to have been chosen because it was Hitler's birthday. It is so sad. So depressing. I laughingly say, "I always knew school wasn't healthy for children, " and I feel, but don't say, "There but for fortune..."

23 April

I feel in tune with Judaism as sociology, and Zen notions as psychology. To the extent that both are "spiritual," i.e., relate to a larger force, they can work in tandem. Judaism's emphasis on the behavioral and moral, with motivation and intention the only internal issues, maps a meaningful way of life to a point. Mindfulness and detachment confront the fleeting nature of life and the issue of time from a different angle. They are complementary until you come right up against the existential question. To "who am I?" Judaism responds strongly on the side of the individual. I am, and God is Other. He has liberated me, and I must account for what I do with that freedom. The successful meditator will emerge in another place, which I don't yet understand fully. It is not prophesy, but it seems pretty close to the Maimonedean notion of thought as the ultimate human reality. Nevertheless, both Jew and Meditator would, I believe, recognize some, or much, of the other's ethics and holiness. The Dali Lama's interest in Jews is not only for lessons of survival in exile. It is for the experience of hallowing the mundane, and knitting it into the minutiae of daily life. If every minute is sanctified, then all of life is a meditation, or a psalm. To sanctify a minute, one must be aware of it. The text of Brachot can be seen as words facilitating detachment and consciousness. The blessing recognizes and appreciates God for the moment, but mentions nothing of his own attachment to it. We observe and pay attention to the fruit of the tree, the bread from the ground, or our own existence at an important occasion. But we never mention liking the bread and fruit, or feeling joyful or sad. We bless God on good and bad alike. Is that loyalty and obedience, or is it a smidgen of Zen?

26 April

Meanwhile life moves on, and it seems satisfactory in every possible way just now. Spring is soft and lovely, the kids seem well for the moment, Jay and I have never been closer, more affectionate, or more in tune. I have friends, and time to connect with them. Linda and Jake are coming next weekend. I am disappointed not to have found myself at home in Israel, and that is the loss of a fantasy, but that cannot be that big of an issue...or can it?

27 April

The music of aging plays softly but persistently at the edges of my consciousness. Today my body hurts. Feet, arms and shoulder blades ache, even after a warm shower. I think, "it's probably arthritis," and then smile, remembering the internist who responded to my shoulder pain back in Philadelphia with, "well, you're 29, you know, you have to expect some aches and pains as you get older." I think about going gray to get away from the dye that may be thinning my hair, but I shun the image of sallow skin faded further by a frame of nondescript, gray straight hair. In the gym, I've had enough exercise after burning 237 calories. When I get home I pop those calories back on with a mouthful of cashews. Despite a relatively active life (for a sedentary bookworm, that is), my weight increases. The song of aging gets harder to ignore.

28 April

It's been raining for 13 days, and I feel waterlogged. My very cells are plump with moisture, and my bones object strenuously. I have renewed sympathy for Noah.

I continue to think about - to mull or obsess - about what's next:

I feel like I should be doing more, applying myself more forcefully and in a more focused way, to making the world a better place. But maybe that isn't necessary.

Perhaps it is enough to read books, see culture and entertainment, spend time with friends, and eat good food. To love and enjoy. One can simply splash in the sea, or study a cupful under a microscope. One can organize to protect the seas from pollution, or be a lifeguard at water's edge. Is it merely a matter of taste, this difference between marine biologist and Sunday splasher? The sea, after all, remains indifferent. Does one pick a role based on what feels good? Is it better to be one than the other? Which? Or is the best answer, "all of the above"?

This morning I started off my day by exercising along the Potomac instead of in the gym. Empty green laundry bag in my hand (I had efficiently dropped off the dry cleaning and mailed the kids' Mother's Day card to Grandma.), I strode along river's edge, appreciating the view of the sturdy Memorial bridge, its underside arches looking more European than usual in today's thick, cloudy light. Yellow and purple pansies framing the Watergate greeted me as I walked by. They nodded their agreement with my choice to move through space outside in the world rather than sweating on a machine in the basement.

Gardeners planted unimpressive seeds that exploded into the delight of those colors. Perhaps we look to God the way the flowers look to the gardeners. He planted some seeds of a species and then watches as they continually pour forth creativity in a stream of words and music and images and motion, of healing and building, kindness and thought, of laughter and warfare; demanding, raging, embracing. The stream of creativity flows on - exploring, exporting, encircling, innovating, preserving, restoring, worshiping, amusing, befriending. All from a couple of seeds.

I don't like running; since I don't walk straight, running hurts. Despite my long legs, I have never been been fast or had much endurance. Running broadcasts my imperfections. So I walk. Purposefully, with long, loose strides I go, feeling a smile grow on my face, a slight ache glimmer in my right ankle. That's how I began my day.

29 April

It's erev Yom Haatzmaut (Israeli Independence Day), and the media are full of stories. Mostly about how Israel is a country of conflict, of problems, of dreams unfulfilled. Amos Oz wrote an essay in the Post in which he was proud that Israel is not Scandinavia. It is a loud, noisy country filled with multiple minorities, and 6 million popes (each of whom believes his opinions are infallible). I wish the articles and TV pieces were not so negative. They should read, 50 years—and we're alive! 50 years, who'da thunk? After 2,000 years of not-being, and murdered almost to extinction, we've been back for the past 50! The "even-handed" stories miss the point. It's a birthday, not an exam. Israel should be celebrated, not evaluated. Is the anniversary the right time to analyze a couple's relationship, or the time to raise a glass and drink l'chaim? I'd like to see a story comparing Israel with other 50-year-old countries. With Jordan, with India. How much blood has been shed in each and why? How're they all doing on literacy, universal health care, assimilating new immigrants? Instead we hear, over and over, about the conflict between religious and secular, the failure of the peace process, Rabin's assassination. Can't anyone give us a break?

May

4 May

On a day like today, everything seems possible. The roads are framed by trees in bloom. They wear their full dress green proudly, like soldiers just after basic training. And like soldiers who haven't seen combat, they seem strong, yet young, tender.

Xeriqua was just accepted to a special photo seminar in Oaxaca, Mexico. I've begun to check out the Jewish travel guide, since she will be there over Shavuot. Last night we looked at condos with Elon. The R.s looked well and happy at lunch in Rockville. They were freshly shorn and hairdressed, since today is Lag B'Omer (a holiday that is a break in the weeks of symbolic mourning between Passover and Shavuot; observant Jews refrain from cutting their hair and holding public festivities during those weeks).

5 May

What makes us move on in life? Is it dissatisfaction? Is it yearning? Does a flower reaching for the sun think, "if only I could get a little warmer, a little brighter"? Or does it merely focus on the pleasure of sunning, and find that it has simply become a greater flower in the process?

On self-improvement

Judging from bookstore inventories, and television commercials, Americans are in a frenzy for self-improvement. Experts advise trying harder, or not trying at all. People discuss their eating habits, latest efforts to change, newest discipline tried...and failed. I am often reminded of the moment in *Annie Hall* when Woody's California-transplanted friend zips up his white space suit and explains conspiratorially, "you never grow old."

People in their 30's used to bore me with their concerns: mortgages, health insurance. Now I hear my fifty-ish peers focus on diet, vitamins, exercise, and I am more compassionate, but no more interested. What both subjects share in common is their source in fear. Thirty-somethings with growing families are consumed with the effort of protecting their families - from all the dangers that threaten. The beasts are poverty, sickness, accidents, failure to thrive. The fifty-ites fear ill health, disability, poverty, old age, death. Both cohorts miss the point. The central challenge is not to be afraid.

6 May

I'm just barely beginning to be able to laugh - but with uncertainty - at my demon. More like my imp. He's a funny-shaped little guy who pops up familiarly when my defenses are down. *I'm not really good at anything* is written in bright white on his purple sweatshirt. He has a paunch, short legs, and bears a faint resemblance to the illustration of Rumplestiltskin in one of the kids' old storybooks. Peeking around a corner he notes my shaky aura, a mood of weak gray, as the signal to begin to taunt. I know it's a game he plays with me, the way an ugly schoolyard bully finds the smallest child standing alone. On normal days I wouldn't even hear him, although he's probably always there. But on the other kind of days...moments...the truth of his taunts seems self-evident.

7 May

It's Friday, one of those days in which I feel particularly inept in the kitchen. With no particularly big plans for Shabbat, I nevertheless did what felt like a lot of cooking last night, with some overflow into this morning. The blondie recipe I downloaded from the internet was a failure, probably because I only casually followed the instructions.

At times like this I feel like a bird - a bird-brain fluttering her wings, alighting here, then there, accomplishing nothing. I'm cooking and writing, and doing neither of them well.

The final menus for us and the family who just had their third child (I'll deliver theirs later today): tomato and rice soup, with snap peas garnish, London broil, herbed potatoes, asparagus and rugulach.

Tomorrow L & family will have seudah shlishit with us: the rest of the soup, gefilte fish, lox, lasagna and salad, cookies, ice cream.

Hmmm, added to the failed blondies, that DOES seem like a lot of cooking!

Shel Silverstein, the author of *The Giving Tree*, *The Missing Piece*, *The Light in the Attic*, and others died today at the age of 66. He seemed to be a guy with a quirky view of the world. His work helped children deal with the world's imperfections, and their own. He even taught that perfection would be boring. The circle in *The Missing Piece* needed his wound in order to make his music. When completed, the circle no longer sang. Silverstein was reported to have died alone, of unknown causes. I moderate a course on *End of Life Issues* at the JCC and just scanned a book written for people with terminal illnesses. When I read mysticism I am reminded of how fitting it is to overcome the fear of death. To just get used to the idea, and be at peace with it. That would reduce a lot of neurotic distress (although one could also argue that neurotic anxiety feeds the fear of death).

8 May

I couldn't wait to get home from the gym this morning, to have the house to myself all day. My appetite for solitude is growing. I was glad to awaken early, inhale the morning light, and get to the gym early. On the way home I noticed an short aged black woman, walking with an aluminum cane. She wore pink pants, and a crown of white panels interconnected by yellow crocheted yarn. I would have liked to take her picture.

When I came back, I read the papers which brought me details of devastation in Oklahoma and Serbia. Although one is a "natural" disaster and the other man made, I am thinking that war and aggression are as natural as tornados. And perhaps just as amenable to reasoned control. Littleton, Colorado is now on page 2. The dead have been buried, school re-opened. Will we ever have a narrative explaining that outburst of death? Then, again, do we understand Jonesboro, Heaven's Gate, Rwanda and East Timor? Why can't any two tribes of a species gifted with reason find a way to share this planet in peace?

I'm looking forward to an hour or two of delicious reading (*Nine and a Half Mystics*, another book I borrowed from the JCC on the honor system I invented and rationalize as my due since I teach there for free), made more delicious because it's done at home in the middle of the day in the middle of the week. I won't even forward my office phone.

9 May

S. always reminds me of our school project in which she covered pages and pages of looseleaf paper with information about Harvey's discovery of the circulatory system, while I presented a lightweight report on nursing, written on small sheets, each taped onto a sheet of construction paper. I got an A, she didn't. She's been angry about the injustice ever since.

Today it occurred to me that my work, manipulative though it was, was the start of a long and important course of study. I examined nursing more deeply a couple of years later as a candy striper, and saw the problem of nurses having no authority. I revisited it again on a more mature level in college, and eventually was professionally involved in consulting to nurses and teaching them. Did her report have such long-term effects? Her report was a product that reflected more respect for authority and the institution, more literalness. Hers was more compliant, more obedient, and took more effort. She grew up to become a nurse.

I called S. to share my insight. I had always felt defensive when she laughed about those reports. She frankly admitted that she hated me at the time. I'd smile with uncertainty at her anger at me for having gotten away with a seventh grader's scam. Of course, it was a scam. But in retrospect, the work had been deep and meaningful for me. Perhaps our teacher wasn't as dumb as we thought.

10 May

Our Shavuot weekend was spent in the old borscht belt atmosphere of the Nevele Hotel in Ellenville. With decor of the early '60's, the Nevele felt like a movie set, complete with extras from Brooklyn. The food was good, basic and plentiful, and the weather was perfect. With time and space to go off by oneself, and relief of the effort of cooking, serving and cleaning, the group was very pleasant. I had a real conversation with M, who is 40 and starting to think about doing something for herself. She shared her feelings in a way she never does in front of the whole family group. E also seemed better, now that she, too, is doing something for herself. Although still intense and incessant, she is more relaxed than she used to be, more pleased with herself. She seems somehow softer, more sympathetic. I guess we all are.

When Jay's father said Kiddush from memory and got to the phrase, "*zaycher l'yitziyat mitzrayim,*" (a reminder of the exodus from Egypt) I understood that the Egypt referred to is the enslavement to one's desires. He is comfortable with his limitations. He accepts his "imperfection," blindness, with equanimity, even with love. "This imperfection is perhaps instead of some others...," he says ambiguously. In other words, "*gam zu l'tova*"(this, too, is for the best). In his case it is not a defense, he really means it. But Jay has a hard time with his parents' aging. They are both very frail. Abe and Mercy keep them going with constant attention and support.

So liberation from Egypt, a land of fear, coercion, and sensual riches, is liberation from passions and addictions. Renunciation, with God's intervention. Then into the desert - a metaphor for emptying oneself as in meditation, and relying on Manna, not on oneself. Finally, receiving the path to enlightenment at Sinai, and traveling on that path into the Promised Land. The path is strewn with obstacles, temptations, dangers, resistance. That's what the rest of the story is about.

I savored that insight, brought to me by my blind father-in-law. He might not be as pleased with it, were I to share it with him.

11 May

Two of the saner students in my class on *End of Life Issues in Judaism* left early last night, because the evening's speaker didn't show, and there were good competing programs at the JCC. The remaining 7 and I spent our time talking about experiences, wishes, and the underlying fears that motivated class attendance. Were I not the teacher, I would have left, too. As the conversation proceeded, the table was piled high with remnants of the students inner fabric of pathology. They whined ("it's not fair that air bags are designed for 5'10" men who don't use their seat belts! I'm a short woman who's VERY careful, a responsible driver, and I could be injured by it!"), they were angry (the docs followed mom's advance directive without asking her if she had, perhaps, changed her mind!), they were paranoid (the doc violated confidentiality by saying, "All of John's test results were good."). I was touched most of all by their desperate loneliness ("what do you do if you don't have someone to give your durable power of attorney to? Where do you find someone?").

I understood, and reflected, that what they were afraid of was dying alone, anonymously, in an indifferent, large, blind system. What we lack is a framework, a place where everyone knows our names. Despite my understanding, I was glad to leave at the end of the session. I felt alienated - and didn't want to feel that I belonged with that group!

Still, I often feel like a misanthrope, happy to leave a social environment for the comfort of my quiet little office. I briefly attended a conference at the Omni Shoreham today. I met a few of the people I intended to, felt anxious and out of place in the hallways of networking, and was glad to be out flagging a cab within an hour. Not for me the lubricated handshake, the keeping up to date. Not for me, the cynical evaluation of another's work, the system hustle. I can't dance the Washington dance. Never could.

Back in my office on this perfect spring day, sunny, breezy, 80 degrees, I have my books and tasks - the largest left undone - I have my radio and my journal. E-mail. Phone. A couple of patients to see. But mostly I have solitude, autonomy, and the inside of my head. My pleasures today came in moments: a walk with a friend, an adult child dropping by to prepare her picnic lunch. The breeze in my dress when I flagged a cab at the corner of Connecticut & Calvert. A serious conversation to help a young person move forward with greater maturity felt good. It felt worthwhile, and hopeful. Like the other pleasures, it felt real.

Many people at the conference, especially those who work for the Federal Government, seem so pressured. Like last week's reception on Capitol Hill, conferences gather people in a group ritual that repels me. I'm so lucky to be able to reject it. And I worry less about where I belong. Belonging somewhere just doesn't seem so important anymore.

12 May

I woke up this morning with "cornucopia" on my mind. That horn of plenty that signifies the abundance of autumn, Thanksgiving, but was associated in my sleeping mind with the basket of Godiva goodies Xeriqua gave me for Mothers' Day. Elon took us out for a most pleasant and satisfying dinner at Suki Moon. He was so pleased to be the host, and so gracious in the role! The food was good, the restaurant's family atmosphere fitting, and the conversation was pleasant, relaxed, and natural. A mother at another table asked her two excited little boys to help her blow out her birthday candles. Glancing at her scene made me view mine in a similar context. We were a particular moment in family life: fiftyish parents, twentysomething kids perched somewhat unsteadily on the threshold, looking foreward toward takeoff. I kissed each of them as we left the restaurant, to thank them for the dinner. Xeriqua had already walked on ahead. "I won't let you get away," I laughed, chasing her.

She let herself be caught, and I thought I saw her pleased smile, like that of a much younger, less defensive, Erica.

Later she mentioned that she had dipped the delicious fat strawberry into the chocolate herself. And she asked if she could shower in our bathroom. It felt like détente.

13 May

The New Books bookcase in our neighborhood library has the expected latest on race, gender and self-help; aging, the environment, and money. Of course there are novels of romance and mystery, epic stories, sci fi, and poetry. The top shelf is devoted to God and religion. I took out the latest from my favorite Jew-turned-Buddhist author, Ram Surya Das. I liked his last one, *Awakening the Buddha Within*, so I'll try the sequel. Then there's a book of dialogue between the French scientist father and his son the biologist-turned- Monk. On the very top shelf was a "biography" of Moses, beneath it the range of Christian and non-denominational spiritual books. Perhaps it's the influence of the coming Millennium, or the aging of us Boomers. Religious concerns and the distrust of institutions seem connected. Our institutions are nearly omniscient, with satellites and computers that can trace your every move, practically your every thought. Kafka felt it, and the world is much more dominated by large systems now than in his day. The *X-files* and Rush Limbaugh both live off the audience's willingness to believe that government is sinister, teeming with harmful secrets. Senator Daniel Patrick Moynihan also warned us about government secrets. One book I took out was written by a former Soviet military scientist whose job was to research and produce biological weapons. He says we underestimate the danger of biological warfare: anthrax and plague in missiles killing millions before we even know what the problem is. Robert McNeil wrote a novel about sabotage in the newsroom. We hear about corporate and governmental collusion against which the individual has no chance. There's no more wilderness where we can escape the reach of this pervasive civilization. So we seek the sacred, in which each person is of infinite value to the only Truth that matters.

The shelf of new books in the local public library is the mind of a people who are more secure and prosperous than any in history. Here we sit in the shade of Micah's date tree and vineyard - and we constantly look over our shoulder in suspicion and fear. Is that madness? Or perhaps those who are not suspicious are just fat and happy, unwilling to confront the real dangers that threaten?

The bookshelf is an oracle, and we must interpret its message.

14 May

Bad dream. Disturbing dream. I was taunted, tormented by some women. I felt like a child being teased - attacked and victimized, afraid, angry, cornered - and yelled back in my own defense, calling them names through sleep-slurred lips. Jay heard my cries and woke me up. I was relieved to be back in this reality. Where was that coming from? All I can think of is the connection to my thoughts of fleeing social situations, and avoiding various work possibilities. Is that what I mean when I say I'm a misanthrope? That I fear hostile attacks? Where could this be coming from? I don't really understand it. And I don't like my vulnerability. I awoke again at 3:30 A.M., thinking I heard a television playing loud. Perhaps it had been coming from outside through the open window, because all was peaceful & quiet in our apartment. It was not a good night's sleep

Then this morning I learned that Xeriqua had not been able to sleep last night either. She finally fell asleep at 3, only to be up again at 5. Her anxiety is understandable. She leaves for Mexico in a few days. More immediately, she organized a picnic with her school friends tomorrow. Rain is predicted.

16 May

Emotion has always been a dilemma for me. The problem of the passions: responsible for both pleasure and pain, nothing would get done in life without them. It can't be desirable to quench the fires of passion; depressives teach us that the very absence of feeling is painful. Pain, anger, anxiety, and fear cannot be avoided. No, the idea is to observe the waves of feeling as they wash over. When you swim in the ocean you know you are swimming. The water, its power - sensual pleasure inseparable from threat - surrounds and dominates. The swimmer can't ever be dry. Though soaked, she doesn't drown. Knowing that the waves will carry her to shore diminishes her pleasure not at all. She can't cling to the beach, nor would she want to, since water is essential for life.

18 May

I've begun to think about religious observance the way I think about working out. Both are lifelong disciplines. The more energy and focus you invest, the more you get out of it. As your (spiritual) muscles develop you can do more, and the exercise (observance, ritual) itself feels good. Mood, self-image and optimism are affected. In both, the presence of relationships and a supportive community makes a difference. Some days, or weeks, are lackluster, but as long as you keep going you're still better off than when you neglect it. And then there are better times when you understand, you feel, you go through and *transcend* the experience. Runners talk about getting past "the wall", when endorphins kick in and provide the "runner's high." Religious ecstasy needs no elaboration.

Both change you, inside and out. Both make demands, entail dietary restrictions, and make you more conscious of small things, like how you move. Both can be performed deeply and well, or in a perfunctory manner, just to get by. People are differently talented in both arenas. There are natural athletes, and uncoordinated folks, but both are enhanced by training. There are jocks, and people who just want to use it, lest they lose it. Some are intoxicated by God, others want only to belong, to keep the ways of their fathers. Those who work intensively, with a trainer, generally make more progress than those who go it alone ("*Asay l'cha rav, ukiney 'icha chaver*" Make someone your Rabbi, and acquire a friend). But not everyone has the potential for washboard abs, chiseled arms, or even a size 10.

It seems clear to me that religious growth is development toward transparency. The religious person becomes transparent, with no dark knots of secrecy or hypocrisy. Arrogance dissolves. The religious person is always humble. The light of religious ideas, the compassion and power from which they arise, become manifest through the practitioners' personality, their words and their works. Thus the conflict of the individual vs. the religious authority (or the group) disappears as both work mutually, becoming one. It is not about preaching or convincing. It is about having the wisdom to know when and how to speak, and when to keep silent. With enough practice, it becomes possible to exercise both the self-control and the courage to act on that knowledge.

Just like firmly saying no to dessert, except when the host baked it herself.

Taking the food analogy further - good people who are not religious are like cake without frosting. Religious people who are not good are frosting alone; sickly-sweet, with no substance.

We choose only the best, a frosted cake, when we want to honor and celebrate.

24 May

Lunch alone at Cafe LaRuche accented my sense of playing the coveted role of mature yuppie. I lunched on salad niciose in the garden, wearing loose old jeans, navy t-shirt, and rubber sandals I bought in Eilat. I sat and ate, reading revised manuscripts for *AQ*, which I brought in a funky purple portfolio that matched my purple eyeglass frames. I felt the part of a genuine Georgetown character, and loved every delicious minute of it!

25 May

When Alan, the landlord, raised my office rent just before my last birthday it reminded me that I only rent the space my life takes up. So far it's been a nearly 50 year lease. The "landlord"'s been generous, giving me access to so much of his property. Like Alan, He can decide at any time either to limit the scope of my activity, or charge a great deal more for the time, or both.

I'm just a renter, just passing through. Good tenants come and go, are pleasant to deal with, and don't damage the property.

June

2 June

It's June, and the interns have returned to DC, like swallows to Capistrano. They will bring their youthful freshness to our lunch table tomorrow. They'll share their eagerness and their tender, earnest conversation with us in exchange for food. That way we will all be nourished and refreshed in the Shabbat manner. I do love summer, and all its manifestations!

4 June

My chest is tight, my spirits low. Which is cause, which effect? I made promises to myself about living more healthfully, and skipped the gym again. Watching the flow of my mood, I stopped at the library to take a page from Garrison Keillor's *Wobegon Boy*, which begins this way:

> I am a cheerful man, even in the dark, and it's all thanks to a good Lutheran mother. When I was a boy, if I came around looking glum and mopey, she said, "What's the matter? Did the

dog pee on your cinnamon toast?" and the thought of our old black mutt raising his hind leg in the *pas de dog* and peeing on toast made me giggle.

7 June

The White House is having a conference on mental illness today. Yesterday, in Brooklyn, Mom's physician didn't understand my request that she be put back on medication, since her old familiar delusional themes were returning. Dr. S.'s hesitation? "She's one of the most alert and oriented residents here. She's not agitated. I don't like my patients to be drugged and sleepy in the daytime. Usually when they begin to get depressed it's because they want to go home." What a remarkable level of ignorance for a practicing doc! She reluctantly agreed to give her a small dose and consult with the psychiatrist. I'll call Dr. S. later just to be sure.

8 June

Working at home on this Monday morning at nearly 11 A.M. I take a moment between answering my e-mail and reviewing manuscripts to feel the significance of June. A.L. called this morning. She remembers my last venture into scuba, the years from then to now, and may even have a perspective on them that she could articulate. I don't fully understand the span from then to now, I have merely lived it.

9 June

This morning Elon went to pick up Shoshana at the airport. He had a bouquet of flowers on the seat next to him.

I sent this e-mail to an old colleague and friend who had recently renewed our relationship:

Hi, Bill,

We had a delightful Memorial Day weekend, with just the right balance of time to relax and low-key things to do. A couple of cookouts, some hanging out by the pool...nothing the least bit stressful. We also went out to the war memorials where "Rolling Thunder" had their events. R.T. is the annual Memorial Day gathering of Viet Nam Vets on motorcycles. They meet to challenge the government and remember the 2000 or so soldiers who are still presumably MIA. It's such a peculiarly American mix of patriotism and anger at the government, of black leather rebelliousness and red-white-and blue loyalty. Not to mention overweight men, some grey-haired, but many far too young to have been in Viet Nam, who are just hoping to catch some of the older folks' "cool." A few years ago I took a picture of one of the "biker babes." She was drinking a beer, enjoying a cigarette - and was pregnant.

Wallace Stegner is a fantastic writer. And good writing is such a pleasure to read! I'm reading *Madam Bovary* now, a classic I somehow skipped, and a great read. Jay and I belong to a book club that is often too intellectual for us, and too fond of 19th century writers, but this was one I had long been meaning to read. I'm also doing a little reading in conflict resolution/peace psychology. I'm trying to figure out whether our discipline has something to contribute to this area. What do you think?

Later on this afternoon I'm going to speak with someone who wants to interview me for a pilot TV show on "Heroes & She-roes". The theme is ordinary people who give to others, and they are interested in my Red Cross work. I am so ambivalent about being the subject, that I get irritated (no, hostile) every time the producer calls. I better get over it, huh, Doc? At least I'll try to behave.

We took a long weekend last weekend to visit Jay's parents up in the Catskills. They have such a good attitude toward their disabilities and are constantly laughing at themselves. When Jay's Dad commented about how pleasant the visit had been and for once there was no big argument, I suggested that perhaps we were all finally maturing. His reply? "You've always been mature, Renee. Maybe **I'm** finally maturing!"

What I'm really trying to say, Bill, is that I love my life. My husband likes the way I look, and is often amused by my ideas. My kids are in pretty good shape and have generally good relationships with me. I am not afraid. I have friends whom I variously respect, enjoy and love. The sun shines daily. I feel good. I catch a breeze by the pool. And have so many books to read.

10 June

It's been a wonderful weekend. Jay and I spent all day Friday leisurely cooking in preparation for our Friday night guests. The okra-rice gumbo turned out to be a big hit, as did Jay's leek salad, and the group of 11 guests interacted in a warm, high-spirited way. We had Shabbat lunch in our building, upstairs at T's. There, in addition to neighborhood guests, were Congressman Barney Frank and others who, like T, work with Congress. The food was delicious once again, and the conversation stimulating, led by a very opinionated Frank. He's a pit bull who cuts down his opposition, but listens when the subject doesn't challenge his loyalties.

Frank mentioned an international meeting of Jewish members of Parliament that takes place at the Knesset every couple of years. The idea delighted me! It integrates the old accusation of an international Jewish group that influences governments and markets around the world (Frank is on the Congressional Banking Committee as well as the Judiciary Committee), with "*Kee m'tziyon taytzay Torah*" (Torah knowledge, i.e., knowledge of justice and lovingkindness, will flow from Zion). Expressed in a secular context, it is the pleasing idea of Jews as propagators and participants in spreading democracy. I love the image.

"*V'hitaneg el Hashem, v'yitayn l'cha mishalot leebchem.*"(Rejoice in God, and your desires will be fulfilled.) Although I read and think a great deal about meditative ideas, I suspect that the foundation of my current well-being is materialistic. Peace, prosperity, good health. My children are growing in a good direction, and I am relieved that they are adults. My mother is safe and in no particular distress. At the moment, as far as I can tell, we are crisis-free. In the past, when things were "okay," I would hear myself whining about feeling under-challenged. But now I am not experiencing the old familiar "divine discontent," even though I am open to the next challenge. More than open; I explore new ideas and new projects almost every week. The difference is that regardless of what I uncover, I am content.

11 June

The temperature's back down to 70, a breeze services our balcony where I quiet my mind reading *The Monk and the Philosopher*, and meditating lightly. I e-mailed G. after finishing his manuscript yesterday. I am impressed with how deeply and extensively he has thought about Judaism in particular and religion in general in relation to peacemaking. In a way it seems to me that adoption is an act of peacemaking. The world seems to have declared war on children. In industrialized countries fully 25% of children grow up in poverty. No other age group is so overrepresented among the poor. It is almost as if children are a despised caste - neglected, abused, rejected, betrayed. They are oppressed and dominated because of their weakness. They are regimented, institutionalized, and marginalized. Then, as they grow into adolescence, they are kept separate from the mainstream, deprived of all but a very few opportunities for meaning.

Okay, so I overstate the case a little. Kids are also loved and coddled, their needs fussed over and met. Nevertheless, there is a kernel of truth in the idea that adoption is a conflict-resolving mechanism. Like all solutions, it emerges from problems and from the recognition that while not everything is possible, much good can be done.

17 June

B. bought an apartment in Rechavia. So begins my generation's journey into old age. For New York Orthodox Jews, I've observed, Jerusalem is Florida. I'm struck by the aging, and I recognize - not without some regret - that I can't join the crowd. The satisfaction of retirement in Rechavia belongs to those who have lived their lives Orthodox and New York. We others are outsiders; visitors, not residents (*ger*, not *toshav*). I feel like the teenager I was once, who watched dancing and cheering Bnai Akivaniks knowing that was not for her.

I have a strong sense of time passing. My circle of birth control pills changes color, and another week has gone by: menus for Shabbat, a plan for the next issue of *AQ*, bills and bank deposits, tuna sandwich lunch, pasta salad dinner, incoming and outgoing, the phone, the fax, the radio talk show.

Time still fascinates me. I am in its thrall. More than anything, it is the main enigma.

20 June

Thirty years ago, I laughed that the unfamiliar sounds of

birds singing early in the morning disturbed my sleep: "damn birds woke me up again!" I'd grumble, amused that I had been able to sleep through the open subway rumbling past my street in Brooklyn, but not through the delicate chirping in Rock Creek Park. Yesterday I woke up to the sounds of birds singing to the sunshine on 25th Street. I awoke happy to hear their blessing, and *conscious* of feeling so blessed. I guess there has been some growth in 30 years. One could call it spiritual growth.

Whenever I read about spiritual practices that expose the practitioner to noxious condition, the image of an old patient, Michael S. comes to mind. It reminds me not to take it all too seriously. Just take what I can from it, and leave the rest. Michael was a cantankerous, difficult man, which was why psychology was consulted. I seemed to have a way with him (my old magic with elderly men), and could jolly him for a little while to work with his chronic pain. When it became too much for him he'd say, "I know what you mean. Mind over matter - 'You don't mind, and I don't matter!'" He was old, lonely and in pain. He died not too long afterwards. I hope I gave him some comfort.

25 June

K. said the secret of eternal youth is to accept everything with love.

I think he may be right. I am reminded of it again and again in my Buddhist reading. I can argue that Halacha is Jewish spiritual practice, but then why are so many observant Jews unhappy, unwise, and unloving? Have we been so collectively injured by our history that our personalities have become distorted, our souls deformed? Or could it be that people who live in the world - in the world of work, and love, of family relations and the competitive marketplace - are thwarted by serenity. Perhaps it is more easily achieved in celibacy and retreat.

28 June

Ft. Lauderdale, Florida: In two days down here as chaperone for the shooting of *The Bull and the Bear* I am surrounded by the excessive materialism, vulgar and ostentatious, that is Southern Florida. Tens of millions of dollars are spent on waterfront homes with boats parked at their side, whose owners use them for perhaps a month each year. The water taxi driver ("tipping is appreciated") pointed out the worst, biggest, or most famous of them, and we passengers ogled, as if at a freak show. At a freak show, though, no one mistakes nature's aberrations for normal or desirable. But we are supposed to *want* endless wealth and consumption, which we are sure would look better on us. We, of course, have taste. Las Olas is lined with prosperity. It is entirely appropriate to be shooting a show about the stock market - engine and reflection of America's blessed prosperity - in this setting.

The skimpy strip of beach in Ft. Lauderdale is intimidated by heavy-footed condos and hotels that tower menacingly over it. There is no bit of space for imagination, or vision, nowhere to run, stroll or be surprised. It is as pathetic as a field made barren by planting the same crops every year. Short-sighted greed destroys the very earth it harvests. The natural relaxation produced by surf sounds, salt air, and sand-between-your-toes struggles for existence in an earth infested with overcrowding, noisy New Yorkers, and over-priced mediocrity. The tension made me constantly hungry.

I am here eating entirely too much mediocre food at over-priced tourist restaurants, and reading about the psalms and tzedakah (charity). Neusner's view of tzedakah as a religious act (regardless of what the givers believe) speaks to me. I have often noted that the most widespread act of faith is the decision to have children. What demonstrates more faith in the goodness and value of life (and by extension its source) than the commitment made to a stranger (and every baby begins as a separate person, a stranger to its parents), to be there for him forever, with whatever energies, compassion and intelligence one has? The atheist may describe the action in naturalistic terms, but it is an act of faith nonetheless.

I continue to be overly concerned with my children. I see them struggling, each in his/her own way, and I am frustrated by my inability to help. That frustration fuels the obsession. Frustration and uncertainty are the best adhesives.

30 June

The conduct of therapy was different whenever I recognized that the patient was simply sharing her narrative than when I looked at it as the presentation of problems to be solved. Pain drives the choice of moment to share the story, but it is not the whole story. Each person's life is a story that is acted, then told and reshaped in the telling and the memory. The therapeutic encounter typically takes place after a trauma, something that calls upon the person's resources and experiences in the story to date. It often requires that the story be reexamined or reframed in order to continue to be coherent. That is both the meaning derived from, and ultimately the reality of, that life.

When I work in a disaster setting, it is much the same. Disasters are public events that challenge the ongoing narratives of individuals and communities. The disaster mental health worker begins the reframing process by listening to the story, validating it and the storyteller both. Without denying anything, the good listener notes the strength, optimism and hopefulness in the tale. And the storyteller grows by hearing her own narration.

That's how the transformation from victim to triumphant, if wounded, survivor begins.

Glossary

Aufruf - a synagogue-based celebration on the Shabbat before one's wedding

Chametz – leavening, a food ingredient that must be completely avoided on Passover
Chumash - the five books of Moses

Dayan – a judge on a religious court

Erev - the day preceding a Jewish holiday
Eicha - the book of Lamentations, read on Tisha B'Av

Galus / Galut - diaspora
Gam zu l'tovah – lit., *this is also for the best*

Havdalah - Saturday evening ritual that concludes the Sabbath.

Havurah - an egalitarian prayer group

Kaddish - memorial prayer for the dead
Kiddush – prayer over wine said before holiday and Shabbat meals
Kinot - elegies, read on Tisha B'Av
Kippot - skullcaps
Knesset - Israeli Parliament
Kohelet – Ecclesiastes

Litvish - Lithuanian-style. Lithuanian academies taught a rationalistic, behavioral approach to Judaism.
Lulav - palm branch

Magen David - Star of David, *lit.* David's shield
Mitzvot – commandments
Nachamu – *lit.* Be comforted
Nisan -The month in which Passover occurs

Pesach - Passover
Peyot - sidelocks

Rashi – 11th century French commentator on the Torah
Rechavia - a neighborhood in Jerusalem
Rosh Hashanah - the Jewish New Year

Seder - the Passover holiday ritual and meal
Shabbat -the Sabbath
Shavuot - Pentacost, the Feast of Weeks
Seudah shlishit - supper, eaten late Shabbat afternoon
Shiurim - lectures, study groups
Shiva Minyan - a quorum gathered in the home of a mourner to enable him to recite Kaddish
Shul - synagogue

Shofar - ram's horn
Siddur - prayer book

Talitot - prayer shawls
Tephillin - phylacteries
Tisha B'Av – *lit.* the ninth day in the month of Av
Tishrei - the month in which Rosh Hashanah occurs
Tzedakah - charity
Tzom Gedalia -a minor fast day occurring on the third day of
Tishrei, the day after Rosh Hashanah

Vidui – confession, an essential part of Rosh Hashanah and Yom Kippur liturgies.

Yichus - inherited family status
Yom Haatzmaut - Israeli Independence Day

About the author

Renee Garfinkel received her Ph.D. in clinical psychology from the University of Lund in Sweden in 1975. She joined the University of Pennsylvania Medical School faculty and the University's Graduate Hospital as a psychologist with a specialty in gerontology. After nearly 20 years in gerontology, Renee founded and edited *Adoption Quarterly*, the first peer reviewed academic journal in the field of adoption. In 1991 Renee joined the Red Cross disaster mental health unit assigned to plane crash and natural disasters sites. Renee lives in Washington, D.C. where she has a private therapy practice and is a member of the faculty of George Washington University's Institute for Crisis, Disaster, and Risk Management. She is listed in *Who's Who of American Women and* serves on the Boards of a number of Jewish community organizations.